DAYS OF WAR AND ROSES

Understanding the Prophetic Significance of the Days in Which We Live

BY

DR. RUSS MOYER

McDougal & Associates is an organization dedicated to the
spreading the Gospel of the Lord Jesus Christ to as many
people as possible in the shortest time possible.

Published by:

McDougal & Associates
18896 Greenwell Springs Road
Greenwell Springs, LA 70739

www.thepublishedword.com

ISBN: 978-1-940461-80-9

Printed on demand in the U.S., the U.K. and Australia
For Worldwide Distribution

Presented To:

_____

By:

_____

On:

_____

Message:

_____

_____

_____

_____

Foreword by Bishop Bill Hamon

Dr. Russ Moyer has written one of the most enlightening and challenging books you have ever read. But do not read this book unless you are willing to accept truth and be conformed to the nature and character of Christ. In it, you will discover the times in which we live, revealed by signs in the heavens, prophecies and typologies from the Bible.

I can relate to and understand what Russ is declaring about the Gospel and the Kingdom. The happenings he refers to are real and applicable to the teachings he presents. For sixty years now, I have been a teacher of restoration for the Church and God's present purpose for our generation. The journey of the children of Israel from Egypt to Canaan typifies the restoration of the Church from Martin Luther and the Protestant movement in 1517 until the Prophetic-Apostolic movement in the 1980s and 90s that crossed the Church over its Jordan river. The Saints movement of 2007 got the Church organized and prepared for the warfare they would fight in Canaan to make it the Kingdom of Israel. The third reformation that Heaven decreed to begin on Earth in 2008 launched Israel into the war that God had destined them to fight. We, the Church, are now declaring and demonstrating the Kingdom as warriors in God's World War III.

Dr. Russ Moyer uses different illustrations to bring out the truth that we have entered the prophetic end-times. The apostle Paul declared in Ephesians 1:10 that it is, *"the dispensation of the fulness of the times."* We have entered a new era of Christianity in which there is an emphasis on the Kingdom of God. This is another sign of the end-times, for Jesus declared in Matthew 24:14, *"this gospel of the Kingdom must be preached in all the world as a witness to all nations, and THEN the end will come."* Every Christian should read this book, to receive enlightenment and God's blessings in their life. Thanks and blessings to you, Dr. Russ, for taking the time and effort to make these truths available to the Body of Christ, by writing Days of War and Roses.

Bishop Bill Hamon
Christian International Apostolic-Global Network
Author: **The Eternal Church, Prophets & Personal Prophecy, Prophets & the Prophetic Movement, Prophets, Pitfalls, & Principles, Apostles/Prophets & the Coming Moves of God, The Day of the Saints, Who Am I & Why Am I Here, Prophetic Scriptures Yet to be Fulfilled (3rd Reformation), 70 Reasons for Speaking in Tongues, How Can These Things Be? and God's World War III.**

Acknowledgments

First, I would like to thank my wonderful wife Mave. You are an incredible helpmate, friend, wife, minister, partner and soulmate. I would have never been able to take on this project or complete it without your love and help and support. You were a part of it, every step of the way. During the dark season of my illness, you were by my side, and your tender love and care gave me a very special reason to keep on keeping on. I love and appreciate you more than you'll ever know.

I want to acknowledge the help of Patty Wallace, Ashley Almas, Jessica Williams, Miguel Simon, Linda Cove and Barbara Buis.

Thank you to all the members of the Eagle Worldwide team who helped with messages, PowerPoints, graphics and research.

A special thank you to Linda Cove for the beautiful cover design and graphics for War and Roses.

Last, but not least, I want to thank and acknowledge my publisher, Harold McDougal. You are anointed, talented and gifted for the important role you fill in getting the message on the heart of authors out in the proper form and order. I would never have been able to get through this project without your help, expertise and encouragement.

Dr. Russ Moyer

Endorsements for
DAYS OF WAR AND ROSES

Dr. Russ Moyer, in his new book, *Days of War and Roses,* asks us: "What Time is it? Are you prepared? Are you ready?" We are living in perilous times, times of great uncertainty and unrest. Evil and war erupting all across the globe, and yet we are also living in the best of times.

Dr. Russ teaches that God sets the times and seasons through His calendar, and even though we daily hear of violence in our streets and corruption in our governments, God has set His end-time agenda according to His timeline of the feasts. And He will have His way.

The greatest harvest, the most powerful worldwide revival ever, is upon us, and God is birthing a new thing. Discover in this book how you can align your life, your family, your church and your country to His Word. Glean from it practical wisdom about how you should live daily.

We have great hope knowing that in the midst of great global chaos, God's prophetic timetable is unfolding exactly as He foretold it through His prophets. Rest assured that you have a part to play to bring this end-time harvest in. The labourers are few and yet souls, lost, hurting and broken people, are God's highest mandate. The charge is for the Army of God to arise. Church, our finest hour is ahead.

This book gives us our marching orders, I highly recommend it to every pastor and believer. It will challenge you, inform you and transform your life.

John Irving
Senior Pastor, The Gathering Place
Aurora, Ontario, Canada

In his new book, *Days of War and Roses*, Dr. Russ Moyer gives us a panoramic view of where we are headed in the near and distant future. This book will alert you to attention in this critical time period. Thanks, Dr. Russ, for releasing a key vision into the Church for the days ahead.

Many blessings,
Gale Sheehan
Christian International
Santa Rosa Beach, Florida

Days of War and Roses is a very timely work for the special times we find ourselves in. It is an inspired book with a prophetic spirit, which contains twenty-first century interpretations and revelations that clarify complicated current issues we all face, as kings and priests of the end-time Church. It is a strong call to action from the throne room of God, much like Nehemiah, with one hand on the trowel and the other hand on the sword. It provides the saints and the corporate Church with encouragement and equipping. With its concrete biblical strategies and prophetically-inspired battle plans of love, purpose and spiritual warfare, *Days of War and Roses* is guaranteed to stir the hearts of all end-time warriors. If you let it, this book will serve as a Holy Spirit catalyst to reclaim the lost and launch the saved into the next dimension.

Through an anointed apostolic vision and a strong prophetic voice, Dr. Moyer has placed in your hands a Spirit-filled weapon that will challenge you to step out of what is holding you back and step into your true divinely-ordained purpose and destiny through Christ Jesus. *Days of War and Roses* will allow you to launch and soar with the full freedom of a born-again warrior in touch with your divine destiny.

Dr. Russ Moyer offers a beautiful balance of biblical love and war. If we surrender to Kingdom principles, we will soar with the eagles and be more than conquerors.

Dr. Russell Bradshaw
Pastor, The Refinery
Peterboro, Ontario, Canada

You then, my son, be strong in the grace that is in Christ Jesus. And the things you have heard me say in the presence of many witnesses entrust to reliable people who will also be qualified to teach others.

Join with me in suffering, like a good soldier of Christ Jesus. No one serving as a soldier gets entangled in civilian affairs, but rather tries to please his commanding officer. Similarly, anyone who competes as an athlete does not receive the victor's crown except by competing according to the rules.

The hardworking farmer should be the first to receive a share of the crops. Reflect on what I am saying, for the Lord will give you insight into all this.

2 Timothy 2:1-7, NIV

Contents

Introduction

We are in the "Days of War and Roses." I believe this describes the conflict that is going on in our hearts, the conflict of the last days for the Church. This is the time for kings and priests to arise and go to war. Whether you are aware of it or not, there is a battle going on, a spiritual war, and we must face it with great love and great determination.

In the process of preparation for the great end-time battle ahead, the family of God will be restored as the army of God and trained and equipped by the Spirit and made ready to be launched. We are rebuilding the walls, as in the days of Nehemiah, with a tool in one hand and a weapon in the other.

Part of the contradiction of these days is between what is going on in the hearts of men and women in the world and what is going on in the hearts of believers.

This is crucial to understand as we move into the season ahead. In the midst of chaos and anarchy,

the Lord will make a path forward for us. In other words, these are again the best of times and the worst of times, a time of great battle, but also a time of great victory, a trying time, but also a rewarding time. This is God's time, and we need to get onboard with His program.

Get ready, for in the days to come, there will be continual conflict everywhere between good and evil, even within the Body of Christ. We will experience a strange mixture of times of war and times of love. Get ready for the *Days of War and Roses*.

Russ Moyer
Pensacola, Florida

Part I

What Time Is it?

Chapter 1

Now Is the Time

And that, knowing the time, that now it is high time to awake out of sleep: for now is our salvation nearer than when we believed.

Romans 13:11

Today is a wonderful time to be alive and to know the Lord, for many wonderful things are happening all over the earth. There is a lot of shaking, a lot of moving, and a lot of excitement being felt as everything that can be shaken is being shaken, and many new things are springing forth.

To many, it may not seem like a wonderful time. The whole world seems to be in turmoil, anarchy and chaos. Governmental systems are being shaken, and life, for millions of people, often seems to hang by a thread. Everything in the earth is crying out that this is the moment the prophets have spoken of. It is imperative that we not only understand what is happening and why, but that we also see our part in it and are moved to action.

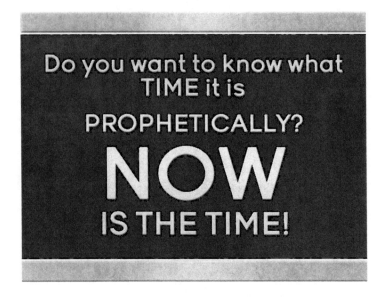

GOD IS ABOUT TO DO SOMETHING NEW

God is about to do something new. A fresh wind is blowing, and it's bringing in something beautiful. You cannot afford to linger in the old because God is doing something totally new. Anytime your memories of the past are greater than your dreams and hopes for the future, you are in a desperate place, and you need to seek the Lord. Your promises for tomorrow need to be stronger than your experiences of yesterday, and you need to get God's promise for this hour.

Sometimes we linger in the old because it felt so good. We prefer to drink the old wine because it tasted so good and we grew accustomed to it. But I'm looking for the new wine, for God is doing a new thing, and this is a good time, whatever others may think. In Eagle Worldwide Ministries, it is a time of rapid growth, re-alignment, shaking and re-setting for the immediate future. Great things are just ahead for all of us. It is time for us to step into our destiny, as God manifests His glory in our midst.

The problems we see in the earth are a result of the Antichrist spirit that is rising up and taking control of many. Terrible darkness is spreading far and wide. But that is precisely the atmosphere in which the Lord promised to send forth His glory upon us and show forth His power through us. As individuals and as a church, we have a great destiny. It's time to let God's glory arise so that our destiny can be manifest. Now is the time, and we must not let it pass.

DON'T PLACE SPECIFIC DATES ON GOD

Nobody knows specific dates for what the Lord is about to do, so don't attempt to put a date on it, but there are indications everywhere that we need to get ready. The heavens, yes, even the entire universe, will manifest the glory of the Lord and bear witness to Him. This end-time season is an important one in which God will manifest His glory in the midst of gross darkness.

Every single day, wherever you look, you can see end-time prophecy being fulfilled. Every time you pick up a newspaper or listen to or watch any newscast, you can see godly principles being attacked by the popular media. Christians believe that their government should function according to biblical standards, that we must get back to the Judeo-Christian values found in the Word of God. Our opponents think otherwise, and the battle is on.

REVIVAL IS JUST A STARTING POINT

Revival is not a destination; revival is only a beginning. It is a refreshing that comes to a weak and broken Church. When revival comes, the Church begins to get stirred and strengthened to join the fight. Now, move out to the front lines of the battle.

The word *revival* signifies that something was once alive, it died and is now being revived. God revives His Church so that the Church can then bring transformation and awakening to the rest of the world. The purpose for revival is to bring the Church back to life, so that the Church can begin to bring cultural change to society. We must re-set society to the norms of the Kingdom of Heaven, re-making the Kingdom of Earth as it was in the Garden of Eden.

The kingdoms of this world will ultimately bow their knee to the Kingdom of God. So a big victory is coming, and we know the end of the story. We win. Our victory is set. Now we just have to stay the course, run the race (whatever our particular race is), and play our part, being our particular piece of the larger puzzle.

A TIME OF ACCELERATION

The Bible speaks of an acceleration of time, and that's where we are right now. We are in a season of acceleration in which technology is playing a major role. If you buy a cellphone today, within nine months or so, it is already outdated, and you feel the need to upgrade it.

The first computer I had for my business had to be housed in a warehouse. It was so big that people would come by just to look at it. And that wasn't so very long ago. Now, however, your most recent smart phone is more powerful than those original computers. Computers now connect us with the entire world, and this is all a fulfillment of end-time prophecy.

Look at what's happening in the Middle East. Russia, the Bear, is again playing a major role and will continue to do so. There are signs of the end-times in the universe (for instance, the blood moons of 2014). The whole universe is bearing witness to the grandeur, the goodness and the greatness of God.

As scientists study the universe, they are learning what that star was that the magi followed to find the baby Jesus. God has always had His GPS system, but the magi were able to read it and to follow it to the very house where Jesus was at the time. Today, we have other signs to guide us.

THE ANTICHRIST IS ALREADY HERE

In the end, we know, the Lord will do signs and wonders in the heavens and in the earth. We can see some of them even now. Personally, I believe that the Antichrist is already alive but not yet identified. You can tell that he is here because the spirit of Antichrist—anarchy and chaos—is being released in the earth as never before.

The way some people are acting is a clue. The anger they sometimes display is not human anger. One minute they are "off the edge," and then, ten minutes later, they are acting totally normal again. This is clearly an evil spirit at work.

THESE ARE DAYS OF SPIRITUAL HARVEST

What an amazing time we live in! There are many teachings you can get on how the end will play out. To me, however, one of the most important things to keep in mind is that these are days of spiritual harvest. Just before Jesus comes back, the greatest harvest in the history of the Church will be reaped. There will come the great move of the Spirit that the prophets have foretold, and that move of the Spirit will bring forth the greatest harvest ever. You and I have been born for the harvest, and these are days of harvest. The fields are white, ready for reaping.

Wouldn't it be terrible to be sitting in the middle of the harvest field and miss the harvest? Some may not reap because they are distracted, discouraged or depressed. All sorts of things can hinder you. Make up your mind not to let *anything* keep you from reaping.

WHAT A SEASON!

What a season we are in! It is worst of times, and it is the best of times. We are on the threshold of the greatest harvest ever known to man, and, at the same time, we are on the threshold of the greatest battle ever known to man. What I want to be sure of is that I do not miss my season, and my season is the season of harvest.

When I went to Canada in 2000 and began to declare that the winds of change were blowing, that it was harvest time and that I had come to reap fields I had not sown (the reaper and the sower are meeting each other), many didn't want to listen. They said, "Canada is a hard place," "Quebec is a hard place." But everywhere I went, God moved in power, and people were saved, baptized in the Holy Ghost, and received the power and the gifts of the Holy Spirit. Today there are many new churches there as a result.

It's harvest time. In the midst of all the bad things going on, God's blessing will come upon us. Persecution will also come, and you can't run away from it. If you are doing the work of the Lord, you will be persecuted. Jesus said, *"If they have persecuted me, they will also persecute you"* (John 15:20). That's the

26

way it works. But with the persecution also comes blessings.

So, stay focused on the harvest. It will surely come. Jesus didn't say, "Pray for the harvest." He told us, rather, to pray for more laborers for the harvest. The end-time harvest will come whether you are ready for it or not. A farmer sows a seed and gets a plant, and when it's harvest time for that plant, he can't afford to be on vacation. If he is not present and ready to work hard, the crop will rot on the vine.

Don't Be Slothful about the Harvest

Please don't be slothful about the harvest. Be diligent. I can't tell you *when* it will happen, but I can tell you that it *will* happen. Everything that has been prophesied *will* come to pass. Every prophecy from the heart of God *will* be fulfilled. Every word that Jesus spoke *will* come to pass. Hang on and do your part, and the harvest will be reaped.

My job is not to predict when it will happen but to be awake and observant so that when it does happen, I will be prepared for it. My job is not to be in fear but to be in faith, knowing that in the midst of anything and everything that happens, God's hand is upon me, and He will help me to reap. That's a guarantee, so I don't have to worry. The world may be worried, but I'm not worried. If I live, I win, and if I die, I win. So, for me, it's a win-win situation.

Have you lost someone you loved? If they loved Jesus, rest assured that they are in a better state than you today. They're up there dancing on those streets of gold, and here we are down here, worrying about looney toons and their crazy nonsense. Stay faithful, and we will soon join the rejoicing.

THE JOY OF THE LORD WILL BE OUR REWARD

The joy of the Lord will be our reward. David said, *"I was glad when they said unto me, Let us go into the house of the LORD"* (Psalm 122:1). He also said, *"LORD, what is man, that thou takest knowledge of him! or the son of man, that thou makest account of him!"* (Psalm 144:3). Personally, I know where I've been, what I have done and where I am today, and I sometimes ask God, "What do You have to do with me?" His great mercy, grace and love are a great mystery to me. Each day I determine to serve Him to the best of my ability as a doorkeeper in His house.

There is a longing in my heart to one day wrap myself around God's feet like a puppy while He is playing chess in the world and having a good time. There is such peace in knowing that He knows us and we know Him. It's so good to be saved and to be alive today.

OUR BEST REAPING DAYS ARE AHEAD

Our best reaping days are ahead. The best is yet to come. Personally, I know that my best days are yet to come. I have a golden sickle in my hand, and I am determined to reap a harvest that no one has yet seen. I will not be finished until the Lord blows the trumpet, but when He does, I want Him to see my sickle in my hand and to know that I have been reaping in His fields. I want to be where He called me to be, doing what He called me to do. I want to be in the place He will be looking for me, and that is in His harvest fields.

I don't want my meeting with God to be like that of Adam. He was ashamed and covered himself because of his sin. Instead of being happy to see the Lord, he ran and hid. If you are in sin, run to God, not away from Him. He is the answer to and the remedy for all sin. His blood was shed for your sin. The price He paid was because of your sin. The cross He hung on was because of your sin. Run to Him, for He has the answers you need today.

When the fire of God falls and every man comes face to face with the Lord of the Harvest, everything you ever did will be tried in that fire. Was it of God or was it of self? Was it of the flesh or was it of the Spirit? Every man's life will be tried. That's why I want to stay focused on the harvest, and that harvest is upon us.

"WHOM SHALL I SEND?"

In Isaiah's day, when the King of Glory came in and His train filled the temple, He asked Isaiah, *"Whom shall I send, and who will go for us?"* (Isaiah 6:8). He is asking the same of you and me today. If you are in the glory, you're in the presence of God, and you know that His heart is for the harvest. So, there's only one correct answer to His call. Isaiah had it right. He answered, *"Here am I; send me!"* And you must do the same today.

When I come before the Lord, I want to have the same confession Paul had before King Agrippa. He said, *"I was not disobedient unto the heavenly vision"* (Acts 26:19). I want to be faithful to the mandate that God has placed on me, and I pray that not one crumb of it is left on the table, not one seed of it is left on the ground. I want every single scrap God has ordained for me. If you don't want to use your sickle, then give it to me. I'll use it.

"LET NO MAN TAKE THY CROWN"

When Jesus spoke through John to the churches, He said, *"[Let] no man take thy crown"* (Revelation 3:11). Be careful! The world around us is trying to shape our existence, and it is making inroads into the church. Would you go to a bar and drink to get someone saved? Many well-meaning Christians are doing just that. But that's crazy. God's intent was that we be *in* the world, but not *of* the world. He surely doesn't want the world in me, for the world is averse to Him. It is His enemy. The things of this world and the things of God do not agree. Worldly wisdom and godly wisdom are opposites. Do not bow your knee to the world; bow it only to the God of Creation.

When you worship in the church, you're not worshiping to make some earthly person feel good. You are worshiping to send up a sweet aroma to Heaven, so that God knows your heart. You are expressing your love for Him and strengthening your bond to His love.

We are much too man-focused, as if the whole universe revolved around me, my kids, my family and my job. No, the universe revolves around the Son. Stop being so self-focused and start being God-focused. Let His Kingdom come. Let His will be done on earth as it is in Heaven.

We worry so much about pleasing ourselves, our friends and the rest of our world that we cannot please God. I must tell you the truth and help you get right with God, and the rewards of that will come. If you don't get right with God, your blood is not on my hands. It will be on your own hands because you have read the truth, and the truth requires a response—the right response.

SO, WHAT TIME IS IT?

So, what time is it? Now is the time! Now is the time to awake, arise and get busy for God. Don't risk falling asleep now. Wake up, for the clock is ticking. It's time to get up, look at the signs all around us and take action. Start celebrating these *Days of War and Roses*.

Chapter 2

Understanding God's Calendar and His Feast Days

Speak unto the children of Israel, and say unto them, Concerning the feasts of the LORD, which ye shall proclaim to be holy convocations, even these are my feasts. These are the feasts of the LORD, even holy convocations, which ye shall proclaim in their seasons.   Leviticus 23:3-4

To understand the days we live in and what time it is, we must understand God's calendar. There is a Hebrew calendar and there is a Western, or Gregorian, calendar, and the two are very different. We understand our Western calendar better because it uses days, weeks, months and years. Too often, however, we don't understand the Hebrew calendar because it is guided by lunar and solar activity.

The *HEBREW* calendar
and
The *WESTERN* calendar

The Hebrew calendar does not work according to hours and minutes. It's sun rise and sun set.

We are guided by hours and minutes, but God's calendar works according to sunrise and sunset. It doesn't work by specific dates, like our calendar; it works on what is happening in the universe at the moment.

This explains why a certain Jewish holiday can be on one day of our calendar one year and on an entirely different day of our calendar the next year. God will do all that He has said in the fullness of His time, which is not according to the Western calendar, but the Hebrew calendar. We must become more sensitive to His timing.

GOD WORKS ON HIS OWN CALENDAR

God has no problem with us celebrating Christmas on the twenty-fifth of December and celebrating New Year's on the first day of January, but He will do what He does on His own timing, not ours.

I celebrate New Year's twice each year. On December 31st and January 1st, we celebrate in a watchnight service, and I proclaim, along with others, what God will do in the new Western-calendar year. I actually begin my spiritual shift, however, according to the Hebrew calendar on Rosh Hashanah, which is the Jewish New Year.

Right after I come out of our summer campmeeting, I begin to seek God, asking Him what He wants me to do next and what will happen in the coming months. Then I begin to get myself into alignment with His timing for that season. I proclaim what God shows me on our New Year's Eve, but I also proclaim it earlier, at an apostolic conference in November. Why do I do it this way? Because God is working on a different calendar than we are.

Another example of the difference is that the Jewish Sabbath runs from Friday evening at sunset until the same time on Saturday. That is not a normal day on our calendar.

Again, God doesn't have a problem with our holidays, but that doesn't mean that He's will do everything according to our calendar. He will do it according to His own calendar. Let God be God and learn to move with His timing.

"THE FEASTS OF THE LORD"

The seven Feasts of the Lord, spoken of in Leviticus 23, all took place by the lunar calendar, so they change on our calendar every year. There were spring feasts, and there were fall feasts. The spring feasts were all fulfilled in the life of Jesus when He came to earth the first time. The fall feasts, I believe, will be fulfilled in the second coming of Christ and in the raising up of the Body of Christ.

The day the Spirit fell on the believers in Jerusalem in the first century, for instance, was not Pentecost Sunday as many Christians believe. It happened on the Day of Pentecost according to the Hebrew calendar. On that day the disciples and others were waiting, and the power of God fell on them. The day of Christ's ascension also happened exactly in God's predetermined timing and according to His calendar.

Often these feasts are called "Jewish feasts," but they were never only for the Jewish people. The Bible has always called them *"the feasts of the Lord,"* for they are His feasts. Like the majority of Christians, I do celebrate Christmas, but I am far more interested in celebrating the Lord's feasts.

I do celebrate our New Year's Day, which falls on January 1 on our calendar, but, on the Hebrew calendar, New Year's is called Rosh Hashanah, and the date of Rosh Hashanah varies on our calendar from year to year. Usually it comes in September or October, depending on the solar system.

Why is it wrong to call these feast days "Jewish feast days?" Because no one group should ever take ownership of them. They are *"the feasts of the Lord."* When those spring feasts were fulfilled in Jesus' first coming, they were fulfilled on the exact day on God's calendar.

"Why are the feasts of the Lord important and worthy of mention?" some might ask. It's because they are another indicator of the times in which we live.

THE SPRING FEASTS

There were four spring feasts: Passover, Unleavened Bread, First Fruits and Pentecost.

The Feast of Passover:

The Feast of Passover, more often referred

to as simply "Passover," was celebrated on the fourteenth day of the first month of the Hebrew calendar in remembrance that God had spared, or passed over, the firstborn of the children of Israel the night the death angel came to slay the firstborn of Egypt. This feast was fulfilled when Jesus died on the cross, as the Passover Lamb, at the exact moment the Passover sacrifice was being offered in the Temple in Jerusalem. His shed blood became an atonement for the sins of the whole world, so that the curse of death could pass over those who had His blood applied to their hearts.

The Feast of Unleavened Bread:

The Feast of Unleavened Bread was celebrated on the fifteenth day of the first month and was in memory of the escape of the children of Israel from Egypt and God's miraculous provision of bread for them in the wilderness. Jesus, the Bread of Life, fulfilled this feast when He was slain and entombed for all those who would accept His sacrifice.

The Feast of First Fruits:

The Feast of First Fruits was celebrated whenever there was a harvest as a symbol of gratitude to God for that miracle. The Jewish people gave not only the first of their crops but also of the animals born to them that year. When Jesus rose from the dead, He became the first fruits of those who will not see death (see Colossians 1:18).

The Feast of Pentecost:

Also known as *Shavuot* or the Feast of Weeks, the Feast of Pentecost was celebrated fifty days after Passover to give thanks to God for the spring harvest. It was on that day that the Holy Spirit was sent, as had been promised by Jesus, to the disciples who waited expectantly in the Upper Room, and the Church was born.

THE FALL FEASTS

Just as there were four spring feasts, there were also three fall feasts: Rosh Hashana, Yom Kippur or the Feast of Trumpets and Sukkoth or the Feast of Tabernacles. Just as the life of Jesus here on earth revolved around the spring feasts, the fall feasts will be fulfilled in His second coming. Everything will happen on God's timetable, not ours.

The Feast of Trumpets:

Celebrated on the first day of the seventh month on the Hebrew calendar, the Feast of Trumpets, or Rosh Hashanah, was the beginning of the religious new year. It was also a time when a trumpet or shofar was sounded in recognition that we would all one day be called to God's great judgment day. Very soon now, that trumpet will sound, and we will all be called to an accounting.

The Day of Atonement:

The Day of Atonement, or Yom Kippur, was a day for the nation of Israel to seek God's forgiveness and a day in which He would pass the penalty of their sins off onto a scapegoat. It was celebrated on the tenth day of the seventh month on the Hebrew calendar. On this day, Jesus will redeem His people.

The Feast of Tabernacles:

The feast of Tabernacles, or Sukkoth, celebrated on the fifteenth day of the seventh month of the Hebrew calendar, memorialized the days when the children of Israel lived in tents in the wilderness and God dwelt among them. During our Grand Sukkoth, He will again make His habitation with men.

40

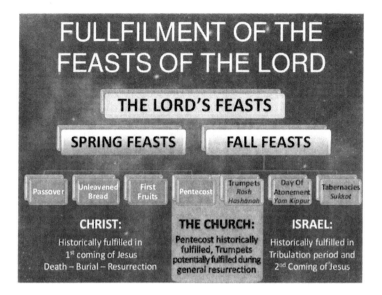

IT'S TIME TO WAKE UP

Just as the first feasts were all celebrated in a short span of time, the fall feasts won't take long to be fulled once they begin happening. Wake up and be ready, for God's time clock is rapidly advancing.

After Jesus had fulfilled the first three spring feasts, signifying His death, burial and resurrection, He remained on the earth for some days, revealing Himself to many. On a single day He showed Himself alive to more than five hundred disciples (see 1 Corinthians 15:6), and yet only one hundred and twenty of these went to the Upper Room to pray and await His promise of the Holy Spirit. What happened to the other three hundred and eighty? Apparently they got caught up in something, were distracted by something or discouraged by something. Whatever the case, they missed their opportunity.

Don't think that they were any different from us or that we're any different from them. We have even more distractions today, more "things" around us vying for our time and our attention, trying to pull us away from the high call of God upon our lives. The enemy loves to get us focused on something that has no eternal value. If he succeeds, we're here today and gone tomorrow, like the grass in the field. We seek God but only temporarily.

LET'S GET SERIOUS WITH GOD

Let's get serious with God. What time it is for you? And what do you intend to do about it? Don't worry about what your spouse does or your sibling does. What will *you* do with Jesus? What *will* you do with His timing? What will *you* do with His season? One day you will meet Him face to face, and you will not be with your spouse or your pastor. It will just be you and Jesus, eyeball to eyeball, face to face.

This *will* happen, and no one will be able to avoid that moment. I'm not talking about your salvation. I'm talking about the testing of the things you have done in your lifetime. Jesus, the Great Judge, will prove our works, so we must always be ready. Make sure you have oil in your lamp. Be prepared for whatever is coming.

Do you remember the Parable of the Ten Virgins? Some of them were prepared, and others were not. Are you prepared? Those who were unprepared were not able to celebrate when the bridegroom arrived. How about you? Will you be ready for what is about to take place?

Just as surely as Jesus fulfilled the spring feasts in His death, burial and resurrection, exactly on time, the fall feasts must now be fulfilled, this time by the Body of Christ. The name, the Feast of Trumpets, indicates that a trumpet will be sounded. The King of Glory will make a magnificent, prophetic utterance, and Rosh Hashanah will be fulfilled. He will declare something in the heavens, and no one living anywhere on earth will be able to say he or she was not warned.

God has spoken through His prophets, but now He will declare His message in the entire universe. A trumpet sound is coming, and that trumpet sound means that God is making an announcement. That's what Rosh Hashanah is all about, the signaling of a change of seasons. And that's where we're headed right now, to the Feast of Trumpets.

FINALLY CELEBRATING

When we finally celebrate the Feast of Tabernacles in its fullness, in the second coming of Christ, we will continue that celebration throughout the Millennium. Don't be disdainful of the earth because it is here that God will form the New Earth, even as He will form a New Heaven, and we will rule and reign here with Him for a thousand years.

God will transform Earth into something magnificent, and here we will celebrate together. These things will happen on those historic feast days, fulfilling all that God has declared. The tribulation period and the second coming of Christ are as sure as the celebration of Rosh Hashanah.

When God's trumpet sounds forth that universal announcement, signaling the birthing of something new, you and I must know prophetically what to look for, what God is doing, and what He now expects from us.

FULFILLED IN CHRIST

The Fall Feasts will all be fulfilled just as Christ prophesied they would be. All that He predicted will happen just as He spoke it. He will come back riding on a cloud, and He will touch down just where He said He would. The army He leads, according to the book of Revelation, will be made up of the called, the chosen and the faithful (see Revelation 17:14).

The final feast, Tabernacles, is a festival of harvest, and the Jewish people have celebrated it through the centuries by erecting and then living for a week in a small flimsy hut, representing the huts they lived in during their wilderness pilgrimage.

Our Grand Succoth will last for a thousand years, a time commonly called the Millennium. During that time, the Lord will dwell with us and rule with us. What a glorious time that will be! Are you getting ready for it? Start celebrating these *Days of War and Roses.*

Chapter 3

Understanding the Signs of the Time

A great sign appeared in heaven: a woman clothed with the sun, with the moon under her feet and a crown of twelve stars on her head. She was pregnant and cried out in pain as she was about to give birth. Revelation 12:1-2, NIV

In the spring of 2017, I became aware of an extremely unusual alignment of heavenly bodies, pointing to September 23 (which happened to be Rosh Hashanah, the Feast of Trumpets, that year), as a day of great prophetic significance. In our universe, things were aligning to reveal the *"great sign"* mentioned in Revelation 12:1.

To me, the shift that happened at Rosh Hashanah was a warning sound, a trumpet sound, so that people who had ears to hear would bring their

September 2017

Sunday	Monday	Tuesday	Wednesday	Thursday	Friday	Saturday
					1	2
3	4	5	6	7	8	9
10	11	12	13	14	15	16
17	18	19	20 Erev Rosh Hashana	21 Rosh Hashana 5778	22 Rosh Hashana II	23 Shabbat Shuva
24 Tzom Gedaliah	25	26	27	28	29 Erev Yom Kippur	30 Yom Kippur

‹ August 2017   Sep   October 2017 ›

lives into alignment with what God was about to do next. This revelation, however, was *only* for those who had ears to hear and eyes to see, for when I began to speak of these things, some initially responded, "What on earth is this man talking about?"

Then, as we began to hear more and more about this very significant event, as other prophetic voices began declaring it and we actually saw talk on secular news about the strange alignment in the heavenlies that was to occur that September, some began to reconsider. I, for one, am convinced that what happened in that September day was the fulfillment of Revelation 12:1-2.

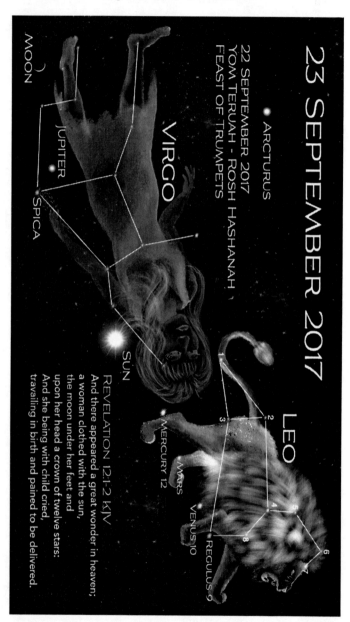

23 SEPTEMBER 2017

22 SEPTEMBER 2017
YOM TERUAH - ROSH HASHANAH
FEAST OF TRUMPETS

ARCTURUS

VIRGO

MOON

JUPITER

SPICA

SUN

LEO

MERCURY 12

MARS

VENUS 10

REGULUS 9

REVELATION 12:1-2 KJV
And there appeared a great wonder in heaven;
a woman clothed with the sun,
the moon under her feet and
upon her head a crown of twelve stars:
And she being with child cried,
travailing in birth and pained to be delivered.

48

THE WOMAN COULD BE SEEN

In the days leading up to September 23, the woman mentioned in those verses could be seen in the heavenlies with Jupiter in her belly, and scientists predicted that she would give birth (that Jupiter would come out of her belly) on September 23. Everything was lined up, and there was no getting away from the fact that God was making an announcement on Rosh Hashanah, during the Feast of Trumpets.

The woman, the constellation Virgo, was there for all to see. Around her head was a crown of stars for all to see. At her feet was the moon for all to see. And there was Jupiter, the King planet, in her belly, about to be birthed. Who could deny it? To me, this signified that the Kingdom of God, for which we have labored and waited, was about to be born.

SOME SAID THAT JESUS WOULD COME

Some people actually said they thought Jesus would come back on September 23. That, of course, didn't happen. However, on September 23, 2017, everything lined up in the heavenlies for us just as it had for the wise men who had a revelation that Jesus was born and were then guided to the spot where He was. The whole world didn't show up in Bethlehem, but a few shepherds did and also a few wise men who understood the signs of the times. They were the seekers, and true seekers are still hearing what God is saying today.

What happened on Rosh Hashanah of 2017 declared a new year, a new feast of trumpets, and God laid it out so convincingly in the heavenlies that no man or woman could ever say they didn't know or that no one had told them.

GOD SPEAKS THROUGH HIS PROPHETS

For centuries now God has been sending His prophets. Then He sent His own Son, and now He is raising up New Testament prophets who are declaring what He is about to do. He will not do anything without first revealing it to and through His prophets. In 2017, He added a voice to the list. If it were not enough to hear it from the prophets, God declared it in the very heavens.

Again, I am convinced that a trumpet was blown that day that resounded around the world. Anyone who had any understanding of the prophetic saw what happened on those days as a major sign of the times.

THE WORD OF GOD IS SURE

The Word of God, whether spoken through the prophets or through the Bible itself, is sure. Every word of it will be fulfilled.

I have traveled across North America and around the world to some two hundred and fifty or three hundred churches of all kinds, and I can tell you that there is a lot of talk and a lot of teaching about the Kingdom these days. Strangely, though I haven't seen many who are legitimately living the Kingdom life. Most of the people I meet are somewhere between Egypt and the Promised Land, still in their wilderness experience, still wandering and waiting for their day of destiny.

Do we have an opportunity to finally embrace the Kingdom? Absolutely, Jesus came preaching that Kingdom, and the fulfillment of His many teachings on the Kingdom are now coming. A fresh new dimension of the Kingdom is being released in this generation, and what we're going to see is Kingdom reality now coming to pass. This is the birthing season, and something is being birthed in the Spirit. If you have ears to hear, then surely you have felt the shift taking place. Surely you have felt the acceleration of our times. Surely you can hear the rumblings going forth throughout the apostolic community.

MY DREAM

Not long before the woman of Revelation 12:1-2 appeared in the heavens, I had a strange dream. In my dream, I was lying in bed asleep, and when I woke up, I was at the bottom of the bed (which reveals the position of the Church today). I looked up, and there was a queen-sized headboard, and next to me was a blonde woman, not my wife. She had on a beautiful blue gown, and I was shocked, and a little afraid, to see her lying there.

Soon, however, my initial shock and fear gave way to a wonderful peace, and I laid my head on the woman's knee. (The Body of Christ needs to come to a place of rest in prayer and intercession.) Then I fell asleep again.

When I woke up, the blonde woman was pregnant, very pregnant. Still, I felt a great peace. Like many men do, I put my head on her belly, wanting to listen to the sounds of the baby. What I heard, however, was not the gurgling sounds of a baby, but the marching of feet. At first, it was the sound of only one or two soldiers marching, but then it quickly became many soldiers marching, a whole army marching together, their boots banging.

Hearing an army marching inside of the woman caused me to know immediately what was to happen. It would be the birthing of an end-time prophetic army, an army of end-time handmaidens and end-time warriors, ready for battle.

What happened on September 23, 2017 signaled a shift in the Spirit. There was a birthing, and the Lord blew a trumpet to commemorate it.

THE TRUMPET ANNOUNCEMENT

By blowing that trumpet, the Lord made an announcement that the Kingdom of God is coming into reality, that there is a fresh new realm of Kingdom, Kingdom authority and Kingdom power that is being released. This is the power of the supernatural Spirit of God, the Kingdom of God made manifest, the glory of God revealed on the earth.

We need to quickly get into the glory realm, the supernatural realm, the realm where anything is possible, the realm where the gifts of the Spirit and the power of God and His manifest presence are experienced. Even as all sorts of craziness is going on in the earth, God is making a path forward for those of us who believe.

If nothing else, what happened on September 23, 2017 was a sign that we should wake up, look at what is happening and realize that the fullness of all things is coming quickly. When God moves, it won't take long. Many prophecies can be fulfilled in a very short span of time. God is doing all that He can to get our attention and make us aware of the time in which we live. Now is the time to act.

JUST A COINCIDENCE?

Was it just a coincidence that this particular alignment of the constellations took place and held their position for more than nine months? Surely this must have been an indication that something was about to happen, something was about to be birthed.

Could it be that a mighty move of the Spirit is being birthed? Could it be that the King is coming into His Kingdom? If not, what does the emergence of this king planet mean to us?

This is not something for us to be worried about. What we need to do is pick up our sickle and begin to reap. The harvest is closer than it's ever been, and tomorrow it will be closer yet. The clock is ticking, and there is an acceleration of time.

But those stars were all aligned for some reason. It was a definite sign, making us all wonder, waking us all up. Time is running out.

GET YOUR PRIORITIES IN LINE

What are your priorities today? Get them right because the clock is ticking. Will you stand up and be a real Christian, doing what you are called to do, using every gift, every talent, and every ability God has given you? If not now, then when will you be ready to manifest your destiny?

So many people are saying, "A prophet told me this and this." Then, when you see them two years later, they are saying, "A prophet said this and this." And five years later they're saying the same thing again. I say, "It's time to get up, put your life into alignment with the Word of God and go after His call. What are you waiting for?"

Is it right for us to sit on our couch and declare that the sky is falling. This isn't a game of Chicken Little; this is life and death. Your neighbors are dying around you, and they don't know Christ. There are people you work with who, eight times out of ten, if Christ came back, you would not see them on the streets of gold. So, what are you waiting for? The time you have is limited and it is now. Use it wisely.

Just a few years ago, I was looking down the barrel of a loaded shotgun. I had stage-four cancer and was told that I needed to set my affairs in order. I had never been sick in my life, but now, it seemed, I didn't have long to live. But God healed me, and I know that He spared my life for a reason. So I can't put that reason off into the future. I know that now is my time and it's your time too.

The time God has allotted each of us is precious, as is His particular assignment for us, His mandate over our lives, the mandate to manifest the present-day ministry of Christ in the earth through the power of the Holy Spirit that He has put inside of us. So, go ahead! Manifest your destiny through the power of the Holy Spirit.

MOVE OUT, ARMY OF GOD!

God has an army of volunteers, with free will, who are saying, like Jesus, "Not my will, but Your will be done." What are you doing for God today? What will you be doing for Him tomorrow? Next year? For the next five years? What have you done for God in the last seven years?

Oh, I'm sure you did something for yourself, but what have you done for God? What have you done for the One who gave His life for you, the One who daily grants you life and breath?

I was once dead in my trespasses and sins, blinded by the things of this world, but God stopped the music and walked into my kitchen, setting me free from drugs and alcohol and other sins and addictions of all types. I owe Him everything, and God is looking for a living sacrifice.

IF YOU SAVED MY LIFE, THEN I OWE YOU MY LIFE

In many cultures, if you save my life, then I owe you my life. Well, Jesus saved my life, so the only reasonable sacrifice for me to make for Him is to give Him my all, and that's what I am endeavoring to do. How about you?

Money represents our time and labor, and God wants us to prosper as our soul prospers. But we need to be good stewards of His blessings. If He is prospering me and giving me a Kingdom mandate, I need to make sure that I steward that properly and am accountable for it, and so do you. God said through Paul:

> *Every man's work shall be made manifest: for the day shall declare it, because it shall be revealed by fire; and the fire shall try every man's work of what sort it is.* 1 Corinthians 3:13

We will even be held accountable for any idle words that come out of our mouths.

What occurred in the heavenlies in 2017, the alignment of five planets, had not occurred for hundreds, perhaps thousands of years, and may never ever occur again in our lifetime. It was a one-time event. Did you hear God's call through it? Did you answer that call?

When this particular configuration came into full focus in the heavenlies, you could see a woman sitting. You could see that the planets were aligned like a crown over her head. As the Scripture described, she was clothed in the sun, the sun being right over her shoulder. The moon, the Scriptures said, would be under her feet, and there is was.

The Scriptures speak of the woman as being pregnant and travailing, ready to bring forth, and in the configuration in the heavenlies on the 23rd of

September 2017, the planet Jupiter was in her womb. Surely, all of this did not just happen accidentally. God put it all in place.

Some have studied Jupiter and noted that it has stripes and a scar, a wound on its side where it has absorbed the blows of asteroids and comets. Does that not sound like what Jesus suffered for us? In all of this amazing detail, God was announcing the coming of His Kingdom on this planet. Start celebrating these *Days of War and Roses*.

I must mention the signs that are increasing all around us. I regularly travel to Calvary Campground in Ashland, Virginia, for my roots are there. When I leave Hamilton, Ontario, I don't see a single

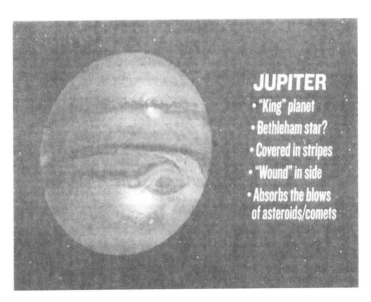

JUPITER
• "King" planet
• Bethleham star?
• Covered in stripes
• "Wound" in side
• Absorbs the blows of asteroids/comets

sign that says "Ashland, Virginia" or even a sign that says "Washington D.C." But after I have driven for five hundred to a thousand miles I begin to see signs for Washington. When I see that, I get excited because I know I am nearing my destination.

It's not until I pass Washington that I begin to see signs for Ashland, and the miles begin to count down: ninety, eighty, seventy, sixty, fifty ... . And I see more and more signs as I near my destination. So why are we seeing more signs now than ever before? Because we are getting closer and closer to our destination.

Expect to see a further acceleration of signs and wonders and a general acceleration of time. Things that used to take a long time will now happen very quickly. Financial blessings will rain down upon us as never before, but it will come, of course, with increased persecution. All of God's blessings come with persecution. There's a war going on, and the enemy will not stop just because you want him to. In fact, even now, he's whispering in your ear, trying to knock you off track. He's desperate, for he knows that his days are numbered.

Satan knows what is about to happen. He's heard all of the prophetic words. He understands the signs. He knows what's going on. Therefore, he is in a place of desperation and will only increase his attacks. There will definitely be an increase in persecution in the days ahead, as the war between good and evil comes to a crescendo. Even now you can hear the sound of both sides rising up.

Chapter 4

Is This the End of the Age?

Surely you have heard about the administration [dispensation, KJV] of God's grace that was given to me for you, that is, the mystery made known to me by revelation, as I have already written briefly. Ephesians 3:2-3

I personally believe that we are quickly coming to the end of an age, meaning that we are at the very end of the dispensation of grace. There have been a number of dispensations, and each one has had a purpose. We are currently nearing the end of the season, or dispensation, known as grace.

When God's New Year came in 2017, we moved from the year 5777 to the year 5778 on the Hebrew calender, and that signified to me, a new dispensation. We were moving from grace to justice, kingdom and the millennium.

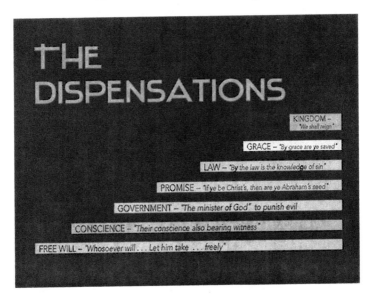

Whether the new dispensation started that day or not, that's where we are headed. We are coming to the end of the Church age and moving into the Kingdom age, coming to the end of the Age of Grace and moving into the Age of Justice.

If you love God, don't be afraid of His justice. He is dropping His plumbline everywhere, to see who is legitimately His. Those who love and obey Him have nothing to fear.

A LEGITIMATE ARMY?

Does anyone imagine that God would call up an army that was not legitimate? Would you? No and neither would He. The remnant, the Bride is coming out of the Body of Christ, and we must consecrate ourselves to the purpose and plan of God. Not everybody will be included. Only those who are serious about the things of God will be called to His side.

THE LAST DAYS

Jesus said that the last days would be *"as the days of Noah"* (Matthew 24:37). In that day, people kept on going about their daily lives while Noah was busy building an ark and telling anyone who would listen that a flood was coming. The great majority of people kept right on getting married, developing friends, attending parties, going to school and everything else under the sun. When the rain suddenly came, they were caught unaware, but there had been plenty of advanced warning.

And that's exactly what will happen again. Many people will never know what has happened, but there will be those who have ears to hear and eyes to see what the Spirit is saying to the Church. These will awaken and advance, knowing that the time has come. It's time, beloved. It's a wonderful time, and we are on the brink of a great spiritual breakthrough.

I believe that the last dispensation is the manifestation of the...

Kingdom / Justice/ Millennium

True believers have been going through a lot these last few years, and I wouldn't want to give the impression that things will get any easier. For us, things will get *better*, but they will not get *easier*. Everything they did to Jesus, men will do to us too.

Some people have actually said, "If it isn't fun, I won't do it." I'm so glad that Jesus didn't have that attitude. Otherwise, He would never have gone to the cross. If the early apostles would have had that attitude, they would never have been dragged through the streets, hung upside down and be-headed for the cause of Christ. What they did was not fun, and if you are determined to have fun, you cannot be part of this end-time army.

God has spoken to soldiers in His Word:

> *Stand fast therefore in the liberty wherewith Christ hath made us free, and be not entangled again with the yoke of bondage.*
>
> Galatians 5:1

Having fun is not wrong. I love to have fun. For instance, I love the manifestation of holy laughter. I got healed through holy laughter. But make sure what you are doing is holy laughter because where we are headed and what will happen over the earth in the days ahead is no joke. The trumpet is about to sound.

COME NOW AND LET US REASON TOGETHER

The Spirit spoke through Isaiah:

> *Come now, and let us reason together.*
>
> Isaiah 1:18

It is time to seriously consider what God is saying. As I noted in the previous chapter, could it have been a coincidence that the planets all lined up as they did on September 23, 2017? Could it have been a coincidence that John the Revelator, when speaking of the end times, pictured the very thing we have now seen in the heavens? Could it have been a coincidence that in the belly of the woman was the king planet? What a coincidence that Jupiter just happened to be there, that the moon was *"under her feet"* and that she was *"clothed in the sun!"* Did all of these elements just happen to bump into each other? Did it all just coincidentally happen at the exact moment of the Feast of Trumpets for the New Year 5778?

Who among us could think that this was all co-incidental? It would take more faith to believe that this was all coincidental than to believe that it was Christ making His announcement: "SOMETHING GOOD IS ABOUT TO HAPPEN, SO STOP MONKEYING AROUND! NOW IS THE TIME FOR ACTION!" Hear the Lord's voice saying, "Now is the time to consecrate yourself, to separate yourself from the things of this world and to fulfil the call that is on your life."

SOME BELIEVE AND SOME DON'T

Some believe in dispensations and others don't. There is such a thing as a dispensation, whether you believe it or not. We have seen the Dispensation of Free Will, the Dispensation of Conscience, the Dispensation of Government, the Dispensation of Law and Promise and the Dispensation of Grace. Each one of these was a different season in history. Now, we are coming to the end of one season and the beginning of another.

In 2017, the calendar of the universe, God's calendar, was at the year 5777, signifying the fullness, the completion, the end of something. Then, on September 23, we moved into the Jewish year 5778, which signifies taking off the old and putting on the new. We are about to make such a dramatic change that I believe this will be the shift in which the sons and daughters will be birthed, and this spiritual shift in the universe will allow the Body of Christ to take a new position and posture—that of the Kingdom of God on earth. We are even now moving into the fulfillment of Kingdom, the next dispensation, the Dispensation of the Kingdom, and we are moving toward millennial rule and reign.

A PERIOD OF TRANSITION

We are currently in a period of transition, moving from the old and into the new, which is the Kingdom in its fullness and then the millennial rule. The Kingdom comes first. This is why Jesus told us to pray: *"Thy Kingdom come, Thy will be done on earth as it is in heaven."* This will all happen right here on the earth.

Something new is going to happen, so prepare yourself for it. We're moving into the Kingdom dispensation, the Dispensation of Justice and Righteous Rule.

Again, don't let this word *justice* frighten you. We don't have to be afraid of God. We need to have *the fear of* the Lord, but we are not *afraid of* the Lord. What He will do is not against us; He is for us—always.

God Is For Us

When God brings justice upon the earth, His gavel will fall hard, but He will judge in our favor. Justice will work on our behalf. Our God will do mighty battle right in the earthly realm. As surely as it is even now occurring in the heavenlies, this battle will come to Earth, and God's Kingdom will prevail. He will bring forth everything that He has promised. Not one word of His promises will go unfulfilled—not one.

The need of the hour is not for God to come into alignment with what I feel like doing—my hopes, my dreams, my goals, my kids, my "stuff." Instead, I must bring myself and everything that I represent into alignment with Him. He doesn't need me; I need Him. I have to know Who the universe revolves around. It's Jesus, not me.

Jesus will come back with fire in His eyes and a scepter in His hand to rule. Some believers are looking for a great escape, a rescue mission, but this will not be a rescue mission; this will be a victory lap. Jesus will come back to rule, but who will come with Him?

> *These shall make war with the Lamb, and the Lamb shall overcome them: for he is Lord of lords, and King of kings: and they that are with him are called, and chosen, and faithful.*
>
> Revelation 17:14

That's us. I want to hear my Lord say in that day, "This is My good and faithful servant." Therefore I must be faithful with what He has given me.

You Can't Take it With You

When the trumpet sounds, you will go out the same way you came in, and you won't bring any of your possessions with you. Then, when you are face to face with God, you will be naked before Him. He will see you just as you are, and everything will be exposed. Get ready for that day.

If our Lord blows the trumpet, and all we can do is shout, "Hurray!," we will have failed. When the trumpet sounds, I want to have a sickle in my hand, and I want to be gathering in every sheaf that I can. I don't want to miss even one.

Are you ready to take a bold step into your destiny by making Jesus first on the throne of your life? Are you ready to start manifesting your destiny in Him? Make a declaration today about the mandate, the call, the message that has been placed on your heart. Determine to be faithful to it.

IT'S NOT ABOUT SENIORITY

This is not about seniority, so it doesn't matter if you've been a Christian for a month or for ten years or more. His eyes are going to and fro over all the earth, and He's looking for those who have a total heart for Him. If your heart is toward Him or you want to re-dedicate your heart and life to Him, just say, "Lord, send me! Take me! I'll go! Here I am, Lord! I'm ready to re-set the priorities for my life.

When I step out, I will be stepping into a new destiny."

God is never early, and He is also never late. We must be sensitive to His presence, move as He moves and move *when* He moves. He is not in a hurry, so we must not be in a hurry either. We must relax and see what God will do.

The Church of our Lord Jesus Christ was born more than two thousand years ago now, and for centuries the preaching and teaching that came forth were about the Church. This began to change about twenty-five years ago, as God began to give us revelation and speak to us through His servants about His Kingdom. The subject of the Kingdom of God has replaced the preaching and teaching about the Church. Why? Because of the time we are living in.

THE CONFIRMATION

Many other signs, wonders and miracles confirm for us this fact. For example, unprecedented floods are coming upon the earth. All of the things that Jesus prophesied, as recorded by Matthew, [1] are coming to pass. The things that Paul talked about when he commissioned Timothy in 2 Timothy 3 are coming to pass. There can be no doubt that we are

1. See Matthew 24

Romans 8: 19

"For the earnest expectation of the creature waiteth for the manifestation of the sons of God."

2 Peter 3:8

"[8] But do not forget this one thing, dear friends: with the Lord a day is like a thousand years, and a thousand years are like a day."

in the end-times, which Paul called *"perilous times"* (2 Timothy 3:1). If you doubt it, just turn on your television and watch the news.

Many people are asking, "Why are these things happening more often these days?" For instance, "Why have we had so many blood moons in recent years?" The answer is simple: When you set out from a distant place traveling to Pensacola, Florida, you will probably not see any signs for Pensacola. But the closer you get to Pensacola, the more signs you will see. Why is there an acceleration of signs? Because we are getting closer to our destination. These are important times, and you and I need to use our lives for what is important. What is God wanting to say with all of this? Are we now in the last day?

ARE WE IN THE LAST DAYS?

Personally I don't think we are in the last days, for many things have yet to take place before the end. For instance, we must see a great spiritual harvest come in before the end. The Temple in Jerusalem must be re-built before the end. And there are other things that must still be fulfilled before the end. (I will give more detail about them in another chapter.) But who can doubt that something is about to happen? We are definitely in a new season.

THE FULFILLMENT OF JESUS' PRAYER

All of these things will happen to fulfil the prayer of Jesus, *"Your Kingdom come, Your will be done on earth as it is in heaven"* (Matthew 6:10, NIV). We haven't yet received the fullness of the harvest of that promise, but we are seeing glimpses of God's glory.

Rest assured that the best is yet to come. There is a fullness of things that is about to be birthed, and we need to be aware of the timing of it in our hearts and to be meditating on how we need to respond to is. What is God requiring of you and me?

I love the passage that says:

> *For the creation waits in eager expectation for the children of God to be revealed.*
>
> Romans 8:19, NIV

This has not happened yet, but it will very soon. The maturity of the manifest sons and daughters of God will come forth in the fullness of who they are in Him and Who He is in them. The Body of Christ will come forth as never before. All of creation is waiting for it. On September 23, 2017, creation made a loud announcement that the sons and daughters of God were about to be revealed, that the Kingdom of God was about to be birthed. Look for it to happen very soon.

MATURITY TAKES TIME

When those wise men and shepherds came to see the baby Jesus, there were not yet any visible miracles or big crowds following Him. He hadn't yet come into the fullness of Who He was. He didn't even start His earthly ministry until He was thirty.

Still, He was the Redeemer and was attacked, when, soon after His birth, authorities decided to kill all of the male babies in the area. Jesus' life was spared because Joseph and Mary fled, taking Him with them, into Egypt. There He grew and matured and prepared.

> *And Jesus grew in wisdom and stature, and in favor with God and man.* Luke 2:52, NIV

In the same way, something's about to happen in the Spirit realm, but will it come already mature and fulfilled? I don't see anything that God has birthed in full maturity. He births us in a baby stage or as a seedling. But the harvest is in that seed, and the prophet is in that baby. It will take time for the seed to germinate, and then there will be a season of growing. You don't plant a seed today and harvest a crop tomorrow. Fruit takes time to develop.

Just as the woman of Revelation 12:1-2 and the woman of my dream were ready to bring forth their child, the Body of Christ is about to be birthed into a brand new season of power and authority. It has always been there, but now we will see the manifestation of it. Why? Because we are moving into the fullness of time, into a new dispensation.

Is This the End of the Age?

God is declaring the birthing of His Kingdom, declaring that it is time for His harvesters to go forth reaping, and His mighty army will soon arise.

The clock is ticking, beloved, and these are the last days. God is shouting, "WAKE UP! WAKE UP!" That is the meaning of the trumpet. That is what it was saying to us in September of 2017. Let the whole universe be awakened to declare the glory of God and His plans and purposes for all ages to come. The hour of fulfillment has come.

I'M NOT SAYING THAT THIS IS THE END

I'm not saying that this is the end. What I *am* saying is that it is a sign for us to wake up to what is happening and to answer the call, consecrating ourselves to the fullness of Christ. The Lord is showing us that the days are now numbered, and He is sending us a new power and a new authority, releasing us into a new Kingdom revelation. He is saying to us, "Now is the time!"

Maybe September 23, 2017 didn't signal the end, and maybe it was not as important as some of us thought, but you are the one who will have to decide that for yourself. You will not be responsible for others: your mom, your children, your pastor. You must decide for yourself, and others will decide for themselves.

It's Getting Closer

Again, as you get closer to your destination, you will see more signs. The signs and the wonders that we are currently seeing in the heavenlies and on the earth and their confirmation through prophetic words are all part of us getting closer and closer to our destination, to our destiny in God as the Body of Christ. Start celebrating these *Days of War and Roses.*

Part II

Time for What?

Chapter 5

Time for Truth

And Jesus answered and said unto them, Take heed that no man deceive you. Matthew 24:4

This is the time for prophets to preach the truth. Jesus said that the season we are in is just *"the beginning of sorrows"* (Matthew 24:8). The glory of the Lord is coming upon us, His end-time Church, so that we can manifest our destiny, which is to reap the great harvest, the one that must come in before Jesus returns.

A REVELATION OF AUTHORITY

What we need today is a revelation of authority. Matthew 24 speaks of two spirits that the end-time Church will face, the spirit of deception and the spirit of offense. These spirits are attempting to bring division to the Church, to rob us of our power. In order to move forward with God's plan for these days, we need a spirit of unity. That's the only way we will manifest His promises.

Therefore, be cautious of prophecies being released these days. All prophecy must to be rooted in the Word of God. Everything that John wrote in Revelation *will* be fulfilled. Everything that is written in other parts of the Word *will* happen. Many things that are being spoken as prophecy today will *not* happen and *cannot* happen because they are being spoken from the spirit of man and not from God.

THERE IS ONLY ONE GOSPEL
WHAT GOSPEL DID JESUS PREACH?

I see a lot of foolishness being preached these days about the Gospel of the Kingdom. I love the Gospel, for it saved me. And I love the Kingdom and being part of the Kingdom. But Paul said there was only one Gospel (see Galatians 1:6-10). When Jesus came and began preaching, Matthew records:

And Jesus went about all Galilee, teaching in their synagogues, and preaching the gospel of the kingdom, and healing all manner of sickness

*and all manner of disease among the people.
And his fame went throughout all Syria: and
they brought unto him all sick people that were
taken with divers diseases and torments, and
those which were possessed with devils, and
those which were lunatick, and those that had
the palsy; and he healed them. And there followed
him great multitudes of people from Galilee, and
from Decapolis, and from Jerusalem, and from
Judaea, and from beyond Jordan.*

Matthew 4:23-25

John the Baptist, when pointing the way to Jesus,
also talked about the Gospel of the Kingdom:

*In those days came John the Baptist, preaching
in the wilderness of Judaea, and saying, Repent
ye: for the kingdom of heaven is at hand.*

Matthew 3:1-2

If you hear a Gospel of the Kingdom preached
that does not include repentance, reject it. When
John preached the Gospel of the Kingdom, He
said, *"Repent ye, for the Kingdom of God is at hand."*
When Jesus preached the Gospel of the Kingdom,
He said the same thing (see Matthew 4:17). If the

Gospel you hear preached doesn't include healing the sick, casting out demons or other manifestations of the power of God, that's not the real Gospel. These signs come to show us that the Kingdom of God is here.

Before He went back to Heaven, Jesus said:

> *Go ye into all the world, and preach the gospel to every creature. He that believeth and is baptized shall be saved; but he that believeth not shall be damned. And these signs shall follow them that believe; In my name shall they cast out devils; they shall speak with new tongues; they shall take up serpents; and if they drink any deadly thing, it shall not hurt them; they shall lay hands on the sick, and they shall recover.*   Mark 16:15-18

This is all part of the Gospel of the Kingdom. When devils come out, the Kingdom of God is made a reality. When people preach that there are no devils and that there is no deliverance, no Hell, no sin and no need to repent, you can know that they are not preaching the true Gospel of the Kingdom.

Some Preach a Perverted Grace

When men say that God gives you grace so that you can sin more, that is a perverted grace. True grace is given so that we can overcome sin. The whole purpose of grace is so that we can have victory over sin.

God desires that we lift up *holy* hands. If the Gospel you have been listening to has no repentance and no holiness, reject it. There is only one Gospel, and that's the true Gospel of the Kingdom, the Gospel that includes repentance from sin and holy living.

Jesus preached the Gospel to sinners so that they could be converted. He did preach a Gospel of love, but true love confronts sin. Jesus did not preach a seeker-friendly Gospel; He preached a life-changing Gospel.

We are creative, as Christ is creative. We are born in His likeness, so we can create a god that we want, rather than accept the truth of Who Christ is and what He preached. He preached a Gospel that confronts sin, and He never once condoned sin. He did love the sinner, but He hated their sin.

"Go and Sin No More"

When a woman caught in adultery was brought to Jesus, He knew that His oppressors were just waiting for Him to say the wrong thing, to break one of their sacred traditions, so He took His time answering. He listened to the Father, and then He said to the accusers, *"He that is without sin among you, let him first cast a stone at her"* (John 8:7). Then, when they had all turned, one by one, and gone away, He turned to the woman and said in very clear terms, *"Go, and sin no more"* (John 8:11). That is the real grace and the real Gospel.

Everything that you are to be free from has to do with your heart. Freedom resides in a heart that is free to choose not to sin. To follow the Ten Commandments is not hard compared to the sin I carried before I met Jesus. But I was set free from all of that by the Son of God through the Gospel of the Kingdom.

When you talk about the Kingdom and you talk about preaching the same message Jesus preached, first find out what that message was. For my part, I want to preach what Jesus preached, the true Gospel of the Kingdom. He said that we are to be *"fishers of men"* (Matthew 4:19), *"the salt of the earth"* and *"the light of the world"*:

> *Ye are the salt of the earth: but if the salt have lost his savour, wherewith shall it be salted? it*

86

is thenceforth good for nothing, but to be cast out, and to be trodden under foot of men.

Ye are the light of the world. A city that is set on an hill cannot be hid. Neither do men light a candle, and put it under a bushel, but on a candlestick; and it giveth light unto all that are in the house. Let your light so shine before men, that they may see your good works, and glorify your Father which is in heaven.

Matthew 5:13-16

That is not seeker-friendly material. That is true *agape* love that turns us from our own way so that we may follow after Christ (and that is the definition of repentance).

SAVED BY FAITH THROUGH GRACE TO DO GOOD WORKS

You have been saved by faith and through grace, to do good works. That's why you were saved, not so that you could go on sinning. The hyper-grace message of today says that you can lie back and do nothing, and God will do it all for you. That's a lie, and that lie will keep you from your harvest field. Rise up quickly and put your hand to the sickle. Take that bushel basket off of your head, and let your true light shine forth. That is what will *"glorify your Father which is in heaven."*

TO BELIEVERS AND NON-BELIEVERS ALIKE

Jesus preached against sin continually, and in every single one of His parables, He confronted men—believers and non-believers alike—by the power of the Holy Spirit. To the believers, those who loved Him, He said, *"If ye love me, keep my commandments"* (John 14:15). He called His faithful followers to accountability and responsibility.

Faith comes by hearing, but so does doubt, and today deception is in the air. If you do nothing and your harvest passes, you will have missed your reason for living on this earth. You were born for the harvest, so don't miss it. Jesus said:

> *Lay not up for yourselves treasures upon earth, where moth and rust doth corrupt, and where thieves break through and steal: but lay up for yourselves treasures in heaven, where neither moth nor rust doth corrupt, and where thieves do not break through nor steal: for where your treasure is, there will your heart be also.* Matthew 6:19-21

Jesus confronted the men and women of His day concerning their attitude about the things of this world. To them, earthly treasures were heavenly, but He said, "Don't lay up your treasures *here*; lay them up *there*." The world is upside down to the Kingdom of God.

In the Kingdom of God, if you want to receive, you give. The world says, "Store up your toys." Jesus said, "You are a fool" (see Luke 11:20). God's Word declares, *"The fool hath said in his heart, There is no God"* (Psalm 14:1). You may admit that there is a God, but does your life bear witness to that truth? If your life does not bear witness to what you are saying, that makes you a hypocrite, and hypocrites keep a lot of people out of church and may miss Heaven themselves.

Jesus also talked about consecration. Looking back at what He preached, we see:

> *Again, the kingdom of heaven is like unto a merchant man, seeking goodly pearls: who, when he had found one pearl of great price, went and sold all that he had, and bought it.* Matthew 13:45-46

Jesus is that Pearl of Great Price. When I found Him, I wanted to sell everything I had to find more of Him. When you find Christ, you will push everything out of the way so that you can have the Pearl of Great Price, for He changes your heart.

BRING FORTH FRUIT

In his day, John the Baptist preached:

Bring forth therefore fruits meet for repentance.
Matthew 3:8

John was not satisfied with talk of repentance; he wanted to see the fruit of it. And that should be our attitude as well. Show me that you have turned away from sin, away from the world, away from self, and are now following God. Show me the fruit of total consecration (consecration is big in the heart of God). When you try to hold on to things, they have a hold on you. Only the truth will set you free.

In every sermon that Jesus preached, He preached consecration, sanctification, holiness and repentance. That is the only Gospel of the Kingdom. If God allows you the privilege of preaching the Good News, then preach holiness and repentance unadulterated, not watered down.

God called me, through Ezekiel 1:2, to a stiff-necked people who spoke the same language I did.

90

He said, "I will give you a forehead like flint," and then He sent me to Canada. It was my first mission field, and the majority of the people there spoke English. God said to me, "I will put something in your mouth that, to you, will be sweet, but, to them, it will not be sweet at all. If you fail to preach this Gospel to them, their blood will be on your hands."

I had a choice to make. If I preached anything other than the pure Gospel, men and women would die as a result, and their blood would be on my hands. If I preached the truth, and they failed to accept it, then their blood would be on their own hands. But if I preached truth and they accepted it, they would soon be dancing on streets of gold. I didn't want any blood on my hands, so I obeyed God.

THE TRUTH REQUIRES A RESPONSE

When I preach the Gospel and, through my preaching, God shares something with the people who hear, it requires a decision on their part, a proper and a right response. When the truth is introduced to your intellect, the truth requires a response. It is the truth that will set us free, so we need to hold on to the truth:

> *And Jesus said, Are ye also yet without understanding? Do not ye yet understand, that*

whatsoever entereth in at the mouth goeth into the belly, and is cast out into the draught? But those things which proceed out of the mouth come forth from the heart; and they defile the man. For out of the heart proceed evil thoughts, murders, adulteries, fornications, thefts, false witness, blasphemies: these are the things which defile a man: but to eat with unwashen hands defileth not a man. Matthew 15:16-20

It's not what's on the outside; it's what's on the inside and then comes out of a man. These are the issues of the heart.

Jesus said that we would be judged for every idle word that came out of our mouth. He not only warned about acts of sin that we commit; He even spoke of the danger of sinful thoughts and sinful words.

ARE THE TEN COMMANDMENTS STILL RELATIVE?

Many think that the Ten Commandments are no longer relevant. They are from the Old Testament, after all. But that is foolishness. Jesus did not come to cancel the Old Testament; He came to fulfill it. Everything He spoke confirmed the Ten Commandments.

The Ten Commandments are not merely the Ten Suggestions. Rather than lower the bar, Jesus raised it higher. He, Who only did what He saw the Father doing and said what He heard the Father saying, lifted the bar even higher. On the subject of adultery, for instance, He said that if a man just looked at a woman and wanted her, it was the same as having her. He confronted sin that is in the mind and the heart.

Some believe that in the twenty-first century, it is now acceptable for a Christian to steal from their neighbor (as long as they don't get caught). But that is ridiculous. If you come to the knowledge of Christ and continue in your sin, it is like trampling the beautiful spirit of grace under your feet. Learn to live by what Jesus, our Lord and Master, taught, not what carnal men teach for their own gain.

In the true Gospel of the Kingdom that Jesus preached everywhere He went, men were confronted about their sin so that they could be changed, transformed in mind and spirit, into the likeness of Christ by the power of the Holy Spirit.

WE HAVE A CHOICE TO MAKE

You have a choice to make. The words of Amos are coming to pass these days. [1] A plumbline is drop-

1. See Amos 7:7-8

ping all over the earth. A plumbline is dropping in Canada, in the U.S., and in the other nations of the world. A plumbline is dropping in my heart and in your heart, in my life and in your life, in my family and in your family. God is weighing the hearts of men and also the hearts of nations. That plumbline is dropping, separating the sheep from the goats. What side are you on? Are you looking for the Kingdom of Man, or are you looking for the Kingdom of God?

Because I was rich as a businessman, the Lord spoke to me through the story of the Rich Young Ruler. This man came to Jesus with seemingly good intentions. He said, *"Good Master, what shall I do to inherit eternal life?"* (Luke 18:18). That sounded good, didn't it? So, what did Jesus do?

Jesus did not just say a little prayer for the man and tell him how easy it was to inherit eternal life. No, He preached the Gospel of the Kingdom to the man, answering, *"Do not commit adultery, Do not kill, Do not steal, Do not bear false witness, Honour thy father and thy mother"* (Luke 18:20). If the Gospel of the Kingdom for that man included the Ten Commandments, then they are still applicable for us today.

This made the young man very happy, and he said, *"All these have I kept from my youth up"* (Luke 18:21). Was this the end of the matter or was something else required? Jesus could have congratulated the man and sent him on his way, but the man had inquired about eternal life, so Jesus had to tell him the truth about eternal life.

Jesus answered: *"Yet lackest thou one thing: sell all that thou hast, and distribute unto the poor, and thou shalt have treasure in heaven: and come, follow me"* (Luke 18:22). With those simple words, Jesus called the man to total consecration to Him, and that is also what He is looking for from us today. This is no joke. This is the true Gospel of the Kingdom.

GREETED WITH SADNESS

With the first answer from Jesus, the man had been very happy, but now, with this second answer, he suddenly turned sad. The Scriptures declare: *"And when he heard this, he was very sorrowful: for he was very rich"* (Luke 18:23). The man had a lot going for him, and many churches might well have invited one such as him to enter into church membership or even church leadership. But Jesus knew the man's heart, knew that he lacked something vital, knew that he loved his money more than he loved God. So, according to Jesus, he had to leave it all, or he could not gain eternal life.

This is the Gospel of the Kingdom. When you hear another Gospel, reject it. This is a such a dangerous time because many are preaching another Gospel.

The Gospel of the Kingdom was not only the Gospel Jesus preached; it was also the Gospel He lived by. The sooner we can get these truths into our hearts and obey them, the sooner we will bear fruit. And this will be fruit that lasts, Kingdom fruit. It's time to change our ways and do God's bidding.

JESUS' LAST WORDS

As we have seen, on the day Jesus ascended back to the Father, He spoke something that is for all of us. He said, *"Go ye into all the world, and preach the gospel to every creature"* (Mark 16:15). How does that relate to those who are not preachers? The Lord is saying to you, "Go and share the good news that Jesus has changed your life. Preach your testimony." That is your most powerful message. Each of us has an obligation to share our testimony anytime we have an opportunity to do so, and if we fail to do that, we commit the sin of omission.

Know who you are, Who you are following, and Who is with you in this race, and you won't end up being someplace you shouldn't be, doing something you shouldn't be doing. Why? Because the plumbline is dropping. Day by day and moment by moment, we are getting ever closer to the time that Christ and all the prophets of old spoke about. So, sound the trumpet in your part of the world, and be ready for the coming of Jesus. Watch and pray that you may be found faithful. This is the Gospel of the Kingdom.

WHERE ARE YOU IN YOUR WALK WITH GOD?

Where are you in your walk with God? What are you doing for Him? What is it that is standing in the way of you receiving eternal life? What is holding you back? What has you in bondage?

God's Word declares in 1 John 1:9:

If we confess our sins, he is faithful and just to forgive us our sins, and to cleanse us from all unrighteousness.

That promise was not written to unbelievers, but to the Church. And, there is no promise of forgiveness of sin if we *fail* to confess. So, the first step to restoration is to confess your faults, your weaknesses. To Whom do we confess? To our Lord Jesus Christ,

Who shed His blood for us and paid the price for
our salvation. Paul taught us:

> *For all have sinned, and come short of the glory*
> *of God.*   Romans 3:23

And how have we all sinned? In thought, in emo-
tion and in deed, we all fall short. This includes
sins of jealousy, envy and greed. Sin, any sin, that
is unconfessed and unforgiven will take us to the
same death as the hypocrite. Why risk such a death
by harboring any sin at all in your heart? Get rid of
it and do it quickly.

There is only one acceptable remedy for sin, and
that is to confess the sin and allow the blood of Jesus
Christ to cleanse you of it. Satan wants to embed a
root of iniquity into your heart, mind and conscience
that will cause you to sin again and again. Jesus
wants to cleanse you of every sin so that it does not
become a destructive lifestyle for you.

You might be a very good person, one who gives
liberally to the poor. But you still need to confess your
sin and allow the blood of the Lamb to do its work in
you. Revelation shows that we are kept by the blood
of the Lamb and the power of our testimony:

98

And they overcame him by the blood of the Lamb, and by the word of their testimony; and they loved not their lives unto the death.

Revelation 12:11

Stop being so concerned about the person next to you, and show concern for your own soul. For relief from sin, there is only one name that you can call on—the name of Jesus. If there is any sinful thought, word or deed in you, let Him make you fully clean today.

The Only Acceptable Holiness Is 100% Holiness

The only acceptable holiness is one hundred percent holiness. Anything short of that is not holy. If you gave me a five-gallon jug for water, and I filled it almost to the brim with clean water but then I put one ounce of raw sewage in it, would you drink from that jug? Of course not. Almost pure is not totally pure.

There is only one holiness, and holiness is holiness. It cannot come to us by our works, but only by the application of the blood of Jesus Christ and the power of His name. And this can come to us only

through the confession of our sins. If there is some-
thing you want the Lord to remove in your life today,
He is right there beside you. He will remove any sin
that you confess to Him in this moment. That's all
that He can do. He is God, and He cannot lie, and
He said that He will remove sin that is confessed to
Him. So anything that you want removed from your
life, lift it up to Him right now in the quietness of
your spirit, and then just give it to Him.

Maybe there is sin that you are not fully aware
of. Let the Holy Spirit search every crevice of your
heart. When He shines light on something that does
not please Him, lift it up to Jesus.

THERE IS A PLACE CALLED HELL

Many no longer believe in Hell, but there is a place
called Hell, and many will burn there. With some of
them, it will not be because they were a bad person
but because they followed someone who was go-
ing in the wrong direction. The closer we get to the
coming of Jesus the more careful we must be not to
miss it.

When lightning crashed and thunder roared over
Mt. Sinai, the Israelites were afraid. Moses told them
not to be because God was revealing Himself there.

100

His presence will keep us from sin and prepare us for living with Him forever. Some think of God differently, as One who would never hurt a soul. I think they have not read the same Bible. When God seeks vengeance upon His enemies, it's not a pretty thing.

A GREAT DISSERVICE

Prophets have often done our young people a great disservice by not declaring all the truth. The very first time I heard Spirit-filled people talking about the end-times my spirit bore witness with what they were saying. We have long known that Jesus was coming back, and the Word of God made that fact plain, but now there was an urgency to the declarations. Jesus was not only coming back; He was coming back soon. He might come that very day or the next. He might come that Sunday or that Wednesday. Over and over again we heard that He was coming "right now."

Being business minded, for me, two plus two had to equal four. Any numbers, whatever they were, had to add up, and that was not happening. I began to say to myself, "Something is wrong here. I know this is not God's heart. If these young people really believed that Jesus was coming tomorrow, next week or next month, why should they go to law school? Should they sacrifice everything they have been training for to get ready for the harvest? If Jesus is coming back soon, should they go to Florida on Spring Break and hang out on the beach?" Something didn't make sense to me. Somebody seemed to have missed the boat.

Now, It's Different

But now, it's different. Here and there you can hear prophetic things being said, and we need to hear more because suddenly it's all unfolding and being fulfilled before our eyes. End-time prophesies are quickly coming to pass, and things are falling into place. This is the season. If you look, you can see it. If you listen, you can hear it. If you reach out, you can feel it. It's time to let God be God.

Some secular voices, such as newscasters, are making declarations about the fact that this is the end-time. Someone who isn't even a believer knows, and yet some believers don't want to talk about it. When you start talking about the end-times and the events of the book of Revelation in church, some tune you out and just sit there like you're coo-coo. A great percentage of the Body of Christ has no idea of what we're talking about. They have no concept of end times, no concept of the warfare to come. They even have no concept of Heaven or Hell. They don't have any idea that the end times are unfolding before their eyes, as they have no prophetic insight.

We sometimes wonder why people are not in church these days as they were some years ago. Could it be because there is no prophetic revelation in the church today? The result is that people have cast off all restraint and begun to go their own way. When people are missing from the church and we wonder why, could it be because no true prophetic revelation is being released in our generation?

Prophetic Nonsense

Because I am prophetic, people send me books about the end time and ask me to read them and then endorse them. Often I cannot. What they have written is little more than prophetic nonsense, foolishness that doesn't line up with the Word of God. And there is a lot of this nonsense out there these days. Be careful what you're listening to and what you're reading. What you allow to come into your eyes and ears goes into your heart. Make sure what you are reading is rooted in the Word of God, and, concerning what you hear, test every spirit.

Just because someone happens to be a respected prophetic voice isn't enough. Go back to the Word and see what it says. Don't risk being out there when the winds are blowing, and the storms are coming (and they come in every life) because the rains fall on the just and the unjust alike. Storms will come in every season, and when they do, you had better be rooted in the Word of God.

GET A GRIP ON THE WORD OF GOD

The more revelation you get, the more important it is for you to have a grip on the Word of God. I like being out there soaring. I'm into dreams and visions and revelations, but the higher you go in revelation the more you need to be rooted in the Word of God and to know how to test everything you hear by that Word. If you have checked something out by the Word of God and found nothing wrong with it, that's fine. But be sure of it. Many have no perception of the time we live in and how to judge what they are hearing.

I want you to know for sure that Jesus is coming back. It *will* happen! I would even go so far as to say that Jesus is coming back soon. I would not say that it will happen today or tomorrow, but all the indicators are that it will be soon. We are the generation that will usher in the second coming of Christ, and there is now an acceleration of events and of time. Things will begin to happen now as never before.

If you believe it, from this day onward, walk in truth. Learn truth and live truth, and one day you will reign with Him who is Truth. Now is the time for truth.

Chapter 6

Time for Love

Love worketh no ill to his neighbour: therefore love is the fulfilling of the law. Romans 13:10

God is teaching us a brand new way to love. Forty years ago, I got saved. Then, twenty years ago, God touched me again. I didn't know how to love. I was so hard-hearted and beat down. I had grown up on the streets, on ballfields and in boxing arenas. Fighting was my life, and I had bruises and scars everywhere to prove it. I was a hardheaded Italian, and my heart was just as hard. I hadn't cried in years. When God touched me, I began to weep, and I wept and wept and wept some more. He was teaching me to love the *agape* way.

As a result of that touch, I had to call everyone I knew—a very long list—and apologize for anything I had done to hurt them because of my lack of love. I could do that now because I felt love, and I could weep with compassion and feel things deeply. I had gotten in touch with my inner self. But what happened to me at that time was even more profound. The truth is that I had lost my first love.

I Had Lost My First Love

After twenty years of being in Christ and going through the "stuff" of life—including a divorce and the trials of business—I had lost the edge of my first love. I was still serving Christ, leading people to the Lord and talking about my salvation, but I had lost the edge. I don't know any other way to say it. I had lost my first love.

Then God sent me to Pensacola, Florida, and there He touched me again and taught me how to love. He took me apart and put me back together again.

Then, years later, I was staring death in the face. I had stage-four lymphoma. I felt the hand of God, and there was no more cancer, no more pain, no more sickness. And, through it all, the Lord continued to teach me about love. This was another depth of His *agape* love, and it went way beyond myself.

LEARNING TO RECEIVE LOVE

God is also teaching us how to receive love. Some of us have known how to give it, but not how to receive it. When I was sick, I couldn't help myself. I couldn't even hold a door open, and I couldn't drive myself around. I had to have others help me do many things, and this made me feel totally helpless. It was a very humbling experience, and it taught me to receive love as never before.

THE CHALLENGE OF LOVING THOSE WHO HATE YOU

Another challenge is to love those who hate you. Do you have that kind of love? Jesus said:

> *Ye have heard that it hath been said, Thou shalt love thy neighbour, and hate thine enemy. But I say unto you, Love your enemies, bless them that curse you, do good to them that hate you, and pray for them which despitefully use you, and persecute you; that ye may be the children of your Father which is in heaven.* Matthew 5:43-45

That's a big order, isn't it? This is probably the most difficult of all of Jesus' commands to follow.

Time for Love

The only way I could come to love an enemy was to see some physical or financial benefit in it for myself. I couldn't do it just because Jesus said for us to forgive.

Jesus knew the hardship involved in loving our enemies. He showed that it is easy to love those who love us, but still He insisted:

> *For if ye love them which love you, what reward have ye? do not even the publicans the same? And if ye salute your brethren only, what do ye more than others? do not even the publicans so? Be ye therefore perfect, even as your Father which is in heaven is perfect.* Matthew 5:46-48

David had problems with his spiritual father and with his own brothers. He had been rejected and betrayed. Then he had problems with his own men. He made a bad decision one day that led to the loss of their families, and the men all turned against him and wanted to stone him. Still, he was able to sing:

> *The LORD said unto my Lord, Sit thou at my right hand, until I make thine enemies thy footstool.* Psalm 110:1

In those words, I discovered a secret that has helped me immensely.

A FOOTSTOOL WILL LIFT YOU HIGHER

A footstool is something that can help you to reach higher, and God has said that He will make your enemies your footstool. In other words, He will put them under your feet so that you can reach a place in the Spirit you could never have reached without their help.

Every time you think of your enemies, thank God for them because He will turn everything they mean for evil into good. He will use your enemies to bless you by putting them under your feet as a footstool so that you can reach a place spiritually and naturally you could never have reached otherwise. There ... that gives you a reason to pray for your enemies and to love them. God will use them for your benefit.

God is teaching me another aspect of love. He is telling me, "You have to fall in love with change." So I am on a love walk, falling in love all over again, this time with change (for more on change, see Chapter 11).

LOVE FOR BELIEVERS AND NONBELIEVERS ALIKE

This love God is teaching us is for believers and non-believers alike. Our obligation to love believers might be more obvious. The newborn babes need lots of love, but every believer at every level also needs love. If I don't love them, then I have no right to lead them.

Our obligation to love sinners may be less obvious, but think of Jesus and what He did for you and me, and you quickly get the idea of how we need to love the unloved and unwanted.

Many Christians make the mistake of throwing a lot of Bible verses at the people they meet. They don't know the Bible, so we have them at a disadvantage. This often leads to a fight, and that is not what Jesus had in mind.

USE THE WISDOM GOD GIVES

Why fight with someone on the street who doesn't know God and desperately needs to know Him? What possible good can beating him over the head with the Scriptures do? Is that somehow a victory? You might win the argument, but you will surely lose a soul!

God's Word declares:

He that winneth souls is wise. Proverbs 11:30

Use that same wisdom to know how to deal with the lost. I believe in repentance, but it is the love of God that brings men to that point (see Romans 2:4). Therefore, the very best thing you can do for the lost is to show them the love of God.

If you can show men and women the love of God, what Jesus called letting your light shine, you will turn many to the feet of Jesus. This is a very exciting time, probably the most exciting time ever to win men and women to Christ (see Chapter 25, The Great Harvest). Now is the time for love.

Chapter 7

Time for Forgiveness and Reconciliation

But why dost thou judge thy brother? or why dost thou set at nought thy brother? for we shall all stand before the judgment seat of Christ.

Romans 14:10

After the Lord taught me to love, He then began to deal with me about letting go of every offense. I am positive that this is one of the most powerful spirits we will have to face in the end-time church, the spirit of offense. We can't seem to get over things. We go through the whole process of forgiving. We tell ourselves that we have forgiven, and we tell others that we have forgiven, and still the feeling of offense is there. I will confess that sometimes I have had to say "I forgive him" every day for months before I started to feel it.

Sometimes this was because the person was still doing whatever it was that had offended me in the first place. But you and I have a choice to make. We either forgive others, or we will not be forgiven ourselves. And that's not much of a choice, is it?

We go through all the motions of forgiveness, reciting the related scripture passages, and we do our best to move forward, but years later we find that we have not really let go of the hurt. We thought we had forgiven the person, but the fact that we still can't let go of the hurt brings our forgiveness into doubt.

My Dream about Letting Go

I had a dream in 2017 in which I was sitting on the floor in my living room with my legs folded, and all around me were family members and ministry partners. We were all talking and sharing testimonies, and we were very happy being together. Then, suddenly, I looked down at my left foot, and there was a terrible gash across my big toe. It wasn't bleeding, but there was a big hole in it, and sticking out from that hole was the corner of an empty plastic sandwich bag.

As soon as I saw that bag, I pulled it out, but then another one appeared. I pulled that one out too, but another one appeared right behind it. As I continued to pull each bag out of that gash, another seemed to take its place. And this went on and on. Finally, I reached the end of the bags, but by then I had a lot of empty sandwich bags scattered around me on the floor. I wondered to myself, "How was I ever able to walk with all those empty bags in my toe?"

What Did It All Mean?

What did it all of this mean? We say, "I'm sorry," and we say, "I forgive you," so the bag is empty. But, until we make reconciliation and restoration, the empty bag is still in there. We haven't finished the job, and the residue of the hurt remains and hinders our walk.

What does this failure cause? It causes bitterness to take root in our lives, affecting our marriage relationship, our business relationships and our church relationships. Because one person let us down, we begin to expect that everyone will let us down in the same way. We meet someone new, and things seem to be going well, and then we have trouble trusting them because trust has been broken by someone in the past. This hinders us from stepping into healthy trust-based relationships.

As the dream unfolded, I was thinking to myself, "I need to get my toe stitched up!" But, amazingly, as soon as I got the last of the plastic bags out of that wound, the toe was immediately healed. And what does this mean? It means that you need to let it go. We all need to forgive those who offend us in any way, but then we also need to let go of the offense. If you continue to expect people to hurt you, they will. Reconcile your differences with them and move on.

OUR MINISTRY OF RECONCILIATION

Each of us has been given a ministry of reconciliation:

> *And all things are of God, who hath reconciled us to himself by Jesus Christ, and hath given to us the ministry of reconciliation; to wit, that God was in Christ, reconciling the world unto himself, not imputing their trespasses unto them; and hath committed unto us the word of reconciliation.* 2 Corinthians 5:18-19

RECONCILIATION ... that's our ministry. First, we must be reconciled to God, and then we must minister reconciliation to others.

116

Time for Forgiveness and Reconciliation

There is a difference between restoration and reconciliation. Reconciliation is sitting down and discussing our differences and then going forward unhindered by what is past. Sometimes, however, I reconcile a person and then also restore them. This only happens when trust is restored from the person who violated the trust in the first place.

If a man is unfaithful to his wife and they reconcile their differences and want to restore their marriage, he is responsible to re-establish the trust that has been lost, and she is responsible to give him a chance to prove himself trustworthy. Some reconcile but then choose to go their separate ways. Others just leave without reconciliation or restoration. Is that real love?

JESUS GAVE US THIS WONDERFUL MINISTRY

RECONCILIATION ... this is our ministry. It is also an end-time ministry. Why do I say that? In Luke 4, Jesus showed us that He had come to fulfill the words of Isaiah 60:

> *The Spirit of the Lord is on me,*
> *because he has anointed me*
> *to proclaim good news to the poor.*

He has sent me to proclaim freedom for the prisoners
and recovery of sight for the blind,
to set the oppressed free,
to proclaim the year of the Lord's favor.

Luke 4:18-19, NIV

Did men deserve this blessing? Not at all. Yet Jesus came to save them anyway. This is the ministry that has been handed down to us because Christ is now seated at the right hand of the Father.

What was Jesus' ministry while He was on the earth? The goal of Christ's ministry on the earth was reconciliation, and when He went back to the Father, He gave us this ministry. Say this (and mean it in your heart): "My ministry is the ministry of reconciliation." Yes, the Father committed this ministry to Jesus, and Jesus, in turn, committed it to us.

Paul's description of the ministry of reconciliation continues, and what he says next is helpful. Here it is in the New International Version:

That God was reconciling the world to himself
in Christ, not counting people's sins against
them. And he has committed to us the message
of reconciliation. We are therefore Christ's

*ambassadors, as though God were making his
appeal through us.*

2 Corinthians 5:19-20, NIV

How did God go about reconciling the world unto
Himself? By *"not counting people's sins against them."*
And, since He has committed this same ministry to
us, this is the way we are to go about it, showing the
forgiveness of Christ to others. If we can do this, *"we
are therefore Christ's ambassadors."*

Are you an ambassador of Christ? Then you need
to let go of all offenses. Just let it go! Stop keeping
count of your neighbor's sins, against you or any-
body else.

MANY PASTORS GET HURT

I have been associated with the church now for
many years and have had many dealings with pas-
tors. In the process, I have seen pastors hurt in ways
you can only imagine. I have seen them wounded
to the point of being broken, to the point of having
their marriage destroyed. Still, even in these extreme
cases, the answer is the same. You have to let it go.
You cannot say, "I forgive," and that's it. You have
to reconcile, and then you have to let it go.

After the bag is empty, take it out. Don't let it infect you or hinder your walk with God and before men. You have to get rid of it once and for all. Let it go!

"But I was terribly hurt, terribly wronged," some say. "I was betrayed." What did Jesus say about that? Here it is the New International Version:

> *Remember what I told you: "The servant is not greater than his master." If they persecuted me, they will persecute you also.*
>
> John 15:20, NIV

You are His, and the fact that you have suffered as He suffered confirms that fact. So don't be so surprised when these things happen. If you are really Christ's, then you will have the attitude He had:

> *Jesus said, "Father, forgive them, for they do not know what they are doing."*
>
> Luke 23:34, NIV

Who was it who hurt Jesus? It was the very ones He loved, worked with and labored for. They hung Him naked on the cross and beat Him to the point that He was unrecognizable.

NOT A PRETTY PICTURE

Jesus hanging on the cross was not the pretty picture we often have hanging on our bedroom walls. He was beaten until His flesh was ripped away. His visage was marred. The result was described by Isaiah:

> *He is despised and rejected of men; a man of sorrows, and acquainted with grief: and we hid as it were our faces from him; he was despised, and we esteemed him not. Surely he hath borne our griefs, and carried our sorrows: yet we did esteem him stricken, smitten of God, and afflicted. But he was wounded for our transgressions, he was bruised for our iniquities: the chastisement of our peace was upon him; and with his stripes we are healed.* Isaiah 53:3-5

If all of this happened to Jesus, and the servant is not greater than his Lord, what are you expecting to happen to you? Will all men love you? Jesus said:

> *If any man will come after me, let him deny himself, and take up his cross, and follow me.* Matthew 16:24

This Christian life isn't just a fun walk. You won't find any fun walks in the Scriptures. Jesus chose to do what He did for us, and now it's our turn. We must choose to do what we can for Him. What will your choice be?

THE JUDGMENT DAY IS COMING

Every man, woman, boy and girl alive will one day stand face to face with Jesus, the Great Judge of all things, and He will test our works to see if they have been good or evil. Please take another look at the Bible. Read it for yourself, and reject the deceptions being put forth as truth today.

The Bible speaks of the Judgment Seat of Christ in relationship to forgiveness:

> *But why dost thou judge thy brother? or why dost thou set at nought thy brother? for we shall all stand before the judgment seat of Christ.*
> Romans 14:10

> *For we must all appear before the judgment seat of Christ; that every one may receive the things done in his body, according to that he hath done, whether it be good or bad.* 2 Corinthians 5:10

Time for Forgiveness and Reconciliation

That day is fast approaching, and it's time to get right, time to get ready. We are on the brink of spiritual breakthrough, and God wants to position us for the days ahead. Therefore we cannot allow anything to cause us delay. Whether your problem is with your children, your parents, your teachers, your boss, your spouse or anyone else—whoever it was who hurt you—let it go! And don't just forgive; reconcile the situation and get ready to move on to greater things.

As noted, when we allow unforgiveness to linger, it will affect our next relationships, and that is a shame. It wasn't enough that the devil used someone to hurt you in the first place; now you have allowed that thing to hinder your next relationship, and all because you couldn't let go of the hurt.

If we want to walk in victory, we have to let it go. If we want to go on, we have to let it go. If we want to be ambassadors for Christ, then we must do what He said for us to do, exercise the ministry of reconciliation:

Now then we are ambassadors for Christ, as though God did beseech you by us: we pray you in Christ's stead, be ye reconciled to God. For he hath made him to be sin for us, who knew no

123

sin; that we might be made the righteousness of
God in him.   2 Corinthians 5:20-21

Too many times we go through all the motions of forgiveness with the best of intentions, but then we just can't let it go emotionally because the hurt, pain and insecurity they cause all linger like that empty bag that was in my toe. And that hinders our walk and our ministries and our next relationship.

"Follow Peace with All Men"

There's a big difference between restoration and reconciliation, and we must have wisdom and discernment to know and understand the difference because our Lord has called us to live in peace with all men:

Follow peace with all men, and holiness, without which no man shall see the Lord.
                                        Hebrews 12:14

Reconciliation can bring us to a place of peace, allowing us to walk with people who have wronged us without fully restoring them to their previous position in our lives. I must forgive all, even my enemies. I must love everyone, however, I can choose my partners and my covenant relationships. What I cannot do and still be a disciple of Jesus is to walk in bitterness or unforgiveness.

WE MAY NEED HEALING

We may need healing in this regard again and again, but that healing comes when I let go of the offense. If I start a new relationship and am not first healed, I have walls erected that are sure to hinder me. I may go forward a little and then back up, or I may walk away from the relationship altogether in the fear of being hurt again. If I allow old memories to linger in my heart, they will surely block me from receiving love and from laying a new foundation of trust. I have to let it all go.

If I'm afraid to get hurt again, that means I have not yet been healed from the last hurt. I must be willing to make myself vulnerable again.

I KNOW THE HEALER

Here is the thing to remember about hurt: I know the Healer, and, because I know the Healer, I'm not afraid to get hurt again. He healed me before, and He will heal me again. The Lord healed me of the broken relationships of my childhood and the many abuses I suffered. Therefore, today I have no fear of abuse.

That's not because I want to be hurt again; it's because I know the Healer. If He healed me then, He will heal me again. If He healed the psalmist David, He will heal me, for He is no respecter of persons. Because I know Who the Healer is, I can walk into a new relationship unhindered by the hurts of the last one.

On the other hand, I cannot maintain healthy relationships if I am full of fear. Fear will ruin any relationship. Fear is the opposite of faith and, therefore, the opposite of Christ. Fear will prevent me from having a healthy relationship, so I have to let go of the hurts. I have to stop keeping score.

STOP KEEPING SCORE

It's so easy to keep score, but Jesus said: *"Judge not"* (Matthew 7:1). Then He show us why we should not judge:

> *Do not judge, or you too will be judged. For in the same way you judge others, you will be*

*judged, and with the measure you use, it will
be measured to you.*   Matthew 7:1-2, NIV

We have a responsibility before Christ to judge righteously, reconcile and restore when possible, to live in peace with all men and to go forward, letting go of the past. We have to do all of that because all of that is what Christ did for us.

I have to let it go, and you have to let it go. I have to love everyone, fulfill my mandate, positioning myself relationally and letting go of anything that hinders, and you have to do the same.

The NIV renders Hebrews 12:14 in this way, *"Make every effort to live in peace with everyone and to be holy."* God wants you to be holy, to live holy, to be a real example to the people around you and not a stumbling block to your brother. Why? The writer closed that thought with this stark reality: *"Without holiness, no one will see the Lord."*

The passage continues:

> *See to it that no one falls short of the grace of God and that no bitter root grows up to cause trouble and to defile many.*
>   Hebrews 12:15, NIV

In other words, don't give bitterness a chance to take root in your spirit.

How Many Times Should We Forgive?

When asked by Peter how many times we should forgive someone who has offended us, Jesus said that seven times was not enough:

> *Then Peter came to Jesus and asked, "Lord, how many times shall I forgive my brother or sister who sins against me? Up to seven times?"*
> *Jesus answered, "I tell you, not seven times, but seventy-seven times."*
>
> Matthew 18:21-22, NIV

The King James Version of the Bible renders this last number as *"seventy times seven."* That would be 490 times. Whether it is 77 times or 490 times, who could keep track of it all? In other words, Jesus put no limit on the number of times we should forgive. Why? Because unforgiveness blocks your blessing, and most of us know that. Still, forgiving those who have wronged us seems to be a difficult challenge.

But we have Jesus as our perfect example. He forgave those who murdered Him. And what did He say about forgiveness? He said:

Time for Forgiveness and Reconciliation

For if ye forgive men their trespasses, your heavenly Father will also forgive you: but if ye forgive not men their trespasses, neither will your Father forgive your trespasses.   Matthew 6:14-15

If you want forgiveness for yourself, then you have to forgive others. Do you need forgiveness? We all do. Then you have to forgive.

Jesus' Many Teachings on Forgiveness

Jesus actually did many teachings on this all-important subject of forgiveness. For instance, He said:

Take heed to yourselves: If thy brother trespass against thee, rebuke him; and if he repent, forgive him. And if he trespass against thee seven times in a day, and seven times in a day turn again to thee, saying, I repent; thou shalt forgive him.   Luke 17:3-4

Seven times in a single day! Wow! That's hard, but you must forgive.

And when ye stand praying, forgive, if ye have ought against any: that your Father also which

*is in heaven may forgive you your trespasses.
But if ye do not forgive, neither will your Father
which is in heaven forgive your trespasses.*

Mark 11:25-26

The next time that you go to God looking for for-giveness, remember this. Make sure you are willing to forgive those you have been holding something against, so that the Just Judge can forgive you.

Don't bother to ask God for an exception in your case. He will never violate His Word. If you want His forgiveness, you must forgive others. Period!

UNFORGIVENESS HINDERS OUR PRAYERS

Why did Jesus give this teaching on forgiveness in relationship to prayer? It was because unforgiveness is one of the greatest hindrances to prayer. If you want your prayers answered, you must learn these lessons on forgiveness. Not doing so will hinder your prayers.

Jesus said:

"Do not judge, and you will not be judged. Do not condemn, and you will not be condemned. Forgive, and you will be forgiven." Luke 6:37, NIV

What could be more clear?

When Jesus shed His blood on Calvary, it was for the forgiveness of our sins. He taught this to His disciples beforehand:

> *Then he took a cup, and when he had given thanks, he gave it to them, saying, "Drink from it, all of you. This is my blood of the covenant, which is poured out for many for the forgiveness of sins."*   Matthew 26:27-28, NIV

There is only one remedy for sin, and unforgiveness is sin. That unique remedy is the blood of Jesus Christ. I am dwelling on this point because I don't want your prayers to be hindered, because I am a servant of God, and because I am committed to speaking the truth. The love of Jesus enables us to forgive others, even our enemies. So let it go!

Someone You Can't Forgive?

I would be very surprised if there were not someone who still triggers a negative response in your spirit. We are all human, and we get hurt. But if you are still feeling unforgiveness toward someone who hurt you, and you cannot pray for them, that might

131

be a problem. If I have struggled with this issue myself, why should I expect more of someone else? I say it because I want God's best for you, and the best for you is to forgive.

Why did Jesus speak so much on this subject to His disciples? Because He knew that the making and molding of a Christian leader would require them going through the furnace of emotional adversity. It's not so much the physical things that happen to us in life that shape us but the emotional things that shape our spirit, our personality and our attitude.

Who is it in your life that you need to forgive? What is it in your life that you need to let go of? You may think you have already forgiven the person. After all, you said it a hundred times, and you went through all the things you knew to do to change the situation, and you meant it, but the hurt is still there, hindering your walk.

TAKE OUT THOSE EMPTY BAGS

Right now, take out those empty bags that are still hindering your walk. God will help you. With His love in you, you can not only forgive that person; you can also bless them. Release them with your blessing, so that you can remove all the hurts and pain. Ask the Lord now, by the power of His Spirit, to remove the pain from your feet so that your walk, and your relationship with Him and with others will not be hindered.

From this moment on, keep your eyes on the Lord, not on your enemies. When Jesus was on the cross, you were on His mind. When He was beaten, suffered and bled, you were on His mind. He did it all for you and your forgiveness. Do you want that forgiveness today? Then forgive others. If you are okay with not being forgiven yourself, then hang on to that feeling of offense. The choice is yours, and it's not once and you're done; this is every single day. Let it go and be healed.

If you feel that you can't forgive someone because they have never asked you for forgiveness, forgive them anyway. If you can't forgive them for their own sake, then at least forgive them for Christ's sake. Forgive them for your own sake. Unforgiveness, any unforgiveness, will block your blessing. Now is the time for forgiveness and reconciliation.

Chapter 8

Time for Holiness and Purity

For God hath not called us unto uncleanness,
but unto holiness.   1 Thessalonians 4:7

God is calling us to holiness today as never before. We have already touched on this subject, so I will not make a lengthy chapter, but I must say a little on the subject.

See that no one is sexually immoral.
                  Hebrews 12:16, NIV

When you hear someone say that it is okay to be sexually immoral, you can know that it is a lie from the devil. Refuse to accept immorality yourself or tolerate it in others. If it is immoral in the eyes of God, that's all we need to know. Stop it.

If we want to be godly people, we cannot call evil good. We must call it what it is. Stand up and blow the trumpet.

SEE THAT NO ONE IS GODLESS LIKE ESAU

The verse continues:

> *See that no one is ... godless like Esau, who for*
> *a single meal sold all his inheritance rights as*
> *the oldest son.* Hebrews 12:16, NIV

There are a lot of people who are selling their spiritual inheritance for dollars and cents today. They are trading the inheritance of God for fame and fortune. Like Esau, they may change their mind later, but it was too late for him, and it may be too late for them too.

Esau was rejected by God:

> *Afterward, as you know, when he wanted to in-*
> *herit this blessing, he was rejected. Even though*
> *he sought the blessing with tears, he could not*
> *change what he had done.*
> Hebrews 12:17, NIV

God forgave Esau, but there are consequences for sin. Sin is sin, and sin has a consequence. So, we need to get serious with God and avoid the sins of our time. Rather than give in to sin, now is the time for holiness and purity.

Chapter 9

Time for Faith

But blessed is the one who trusts in the Lord,
whose confidence is in him.
They will be like a tree planted by the water
that sends out its roots by the stream.
It does not fear when heat comes;
its leaves are always green.
It has no worries in a year of drought
and never fails to bear fruit.

Jeremiah 17:7-8, NIV

Great things are about to happen, but in the meantime, we must hold tight to God. When your predicament looks bigger than your promise, it's hard to get your mind off of it and keep your mind and your heart on the Lord. You may be standing there with a promise in both hands, but the predicament you are facing looms large in the natural.

When the leaders of Israel sent the twelve spies into the Promised Land, those twelve men had just seen the miraculous, powerful hand of God doing mighty signs and wonders on their behalf. But as time passed and difficulties presented themselves, along with the sight of the giants living in the land, although the men knew all of the promises of God, suddenly they seemed like midgets in their own eyes. We understand, of course, that they were now looking at things with their natural eyes rather than through the eyeglass of God.

SEEING THROUGH THE EYEGLASS OF GOD

What is the eyeglass of God? It is the prophetic word, the promises God has spoken over you and me, and we must view them by faith. If we can view the world through those promises and not through our actual circumstances, we can have an eagle's-eye view, up above all trouble.

When an eagle gets into full fight, there are no small birds around for him to be concerned about. The eagle flies so high that small birds can't get up there. Therefore the eagle doesn't have to waste his time and energy fighting the small birds. He soars far above them. Too often we waste our time fighting inferior foes, for we want to fight every single battle.

But you have to pick your battles. It's a new season and a wonderful time, a time for faith.

Start Believing

I was born in a small town just outside of Philadelphia, Pennsylvania, called Bridgeport and lived on the street corners. I never had money, and neither did my parents. They lived hand to mouth, week to week and paycheck to paycheck. When the Lord saved me, He told me that He would make me rich in dreams and visions. I had no education or background in business, but God put me into business anyway, and within six or seven years, I had earned more than a million dollars. The power and wisdom of God built something that I could never have done myself, and He did it in spite of me.

After about ten years in business, I was interviewed by the *Norristown Times Herald,* and the interviewer said, "It must have been really hard to make a million dollars."

I answered, "No, the hardest thing was believing that I could do it." Believing is very powerful.

You need to believe what the Lord is telling you and trust Him when what He is saying doesn't seem to make sense to your inner self. Self is nothing but trouble. He or she will get you into trouble every time. Self is crucified when Jesus comes into our lives, but he (or she) keeps trying to sneak back in and take over. Self tries to rob us of our faith. We tend to blame the devil for many things, but the truth is that he is a defeated foe and is under your feet. Self is who you need to deal with, so that you maintain an active faith and trust in God.

I Cannot Fully Comprehend God

I serve a supernatural God, so I can't fully comprehend Him with my natural mind. He's an infinite God, and I have a finite mind, so I can't expect to always understand what He is doing. More than that, I can't always explain Him or what He does. If you only move when you have a full explanation and a logical thought in place, you'll never walk in faith. You have to be able to defeat your own logic, your own intellect, your own education. And those things have all been imbedded in us over time and often create unrealistic expectations that keep us from being led by the Spirit.

The Values of My Generation

My generation, born after World War II, has a very different set of values, and I thank God for what was instilled in me as a child. Those values have taken me far in life. But sometimes we are much too loaded down with facts, and those facts often tell me the opposite of what God is saying. The facts say, "This would be a good time to 'pack it all in,' " but God has something entirely different in mind.

The older we get, the more facts we accumulate, but walking by faith in the Lord brings us wisdom, revelation and understanding from Him to defeat the natural. In the end, it doesn't really matter how old I am because the Great I AM who lives in me can do all things, and I have seen Him answer on my behalf.

I know Him who is called Faithful and True because that's what He is, and therefore I have the ability to trust Him when I am confronted with the things that would cause me to stop in the natural. Even when people tell me "no," He tells me "yes." I listen to Him, knowing the voice of the Lord and the promise of God. He said:

> *The people that do know their God shall be strong, and do exploits.* Daniel 11:32

BEING LED BY FAITH OR FACTS

People of faith in God know how to respond contrary to the facts before them. They are not led by natural expectations, either their own or that of others. They are willing to break all barriers and walk through all obstacles. When they have gone as far as they can go and then take one more step, a step of faith, a step in the dark, that is when God meets them, in their place of faith.

IF YOU HAVE TO SEE IT, THAT'S NOT FAITH

If you have to see something first, that's not faith. It is only faith when you can't see it yet. And you have to know how to walk in faith if you want the benefits of the faith walk. There are great benefits to living by faith.

I hear people saying, "I live by faith," but when I look at their life, it's not hard to see that they are not really living by faith. They're living by their own understanding, they have a set pattern for doing things, and they're not about to vary from that pattern. They always say that they are living that way only "until ... ."

Until their children are grown
Until they are eligible for their pension
Until they have enough money saved up
Until they have paid off their home

But the devil will see to it that their "until," whatever it happens to be, never arrives.

Time for Faith

I have seen people delaying ten, twenty, thirty, and even forty years for their "until" to happen. They genuinely love the Lord, but somehow they are never be able to step out fully in faith. The faith walk requires a complete trust in Jehovah, He who is "greater" than any circumstance of life. We could never explain Him or understand Him with our natural minds. We just have to obey Him by blind faith.

YOU ARE ANOINTED

Faith has many aspects. When I first began to minister, I went down from the platform and began praying for someone who was very cold, and the devil said to me, "You can't help them. You're not anointed." But in that moment God said to me, "Just keep on moving because you *are* anointed."

Are you a Christian? Then you are anointed. When you see sickness, hurt and pain, and you feel compassion on the person and want to help them, you are anointed. Pray the prayer of faith, because you are anointed. Don't just say words. Pray with faith:

Is any sick among you? let him call for the elders of the church; and let them pray over him,

anointing him with oil in the name of the Lord:
and the prayer of faith shall save the sick, and
the Lord shall raise him up; and if he have com-
mitted sins, they shall be forgiven him.

James 5:14-15

Pray the prayer of faith, knowing that God is willing to heal the sick, and He will do it through you. If you have experienced some losses in the past, know that your dry season is over. Your painful season is over. The devil may try to confront you, but he is defeated and is soon going into a thousand-year retirement. In the meantime, he's still hard at work. Deal with him with the spiritual weapons that God has given you. You are anointed.

APPLY YOUR FAITH

This is a good season. Apply your faith, no matter what things look like. We are on the threshold of a great breakthrough, and you can hear about breakthroughs already occurring all over the earth. This is a dramatic season. Be careful not to become entangled with the opinions of people so that you miss what is about to happen. Opinions are like garbage cans: everybody has one, and most of them stink. I don't want to be led by opinions, not even my own. I want to be led by the Spirit of God.

What a time this is! Think about it: God has spared us for this very moment. We are part of His great army, and whatever we had to go through in life in the past, He spared us for this moment in time, this dramatic new season of reaping. Have faith in God, for now is the time for faith.

Chapter 10

Time for Boldness

Arise, shine; for thy light is come, and the glory of the LORD is risen upon thee. For, behold, the darkness shall cover the earth, and gross darkness the people: but the LORD shall arise upon thee, and his glory shall be seen upon thee. And the Gentiles shall come to thy light, and kings to the brightness of thy rising.   Isaiah 60:1-3

This is a very important and prophetic season. It is time for the vision and time for the provision. It is time for boldness, for the camels are on their way to bring to us all that is lacking.

We all believe that Isaiah 60 is a prophetic word for this moment. Verse 6 of that passage declares the coming of the camels:

The multitude of camels shall cover thee, the dromedaries of Midian and Ephah; all they from

Time for Boldness

Sheba shall come: they shall bring gold and incense; and they shall shew forth the praises of the Lord.   Isaiah 60:6

God will fund the vision He has placed in our hearts. If your vision came from God, He will provide for it. He is Jehovah Jireh. He is our Provision, not just our Provider, and He will make sure we have everything we need!

I Want it with Everything

Being an Italian, when I order pizza, I want it just like my faith—with the works on it. I mean it; I want everything. And when Jesus orders pizza, He pays the bill. Get ready because He will be funding the vision. There is always provision for the vision, and it's on its way. Go ahead and order with "the works"! Don't be afraid to put your feet on the ground. Our heavenly General will meet you there.

Now is the time. It is the time to be bold and courageous. Now is the time to cross-over Jordan and possess the land. It won't be done if there is a spirit of timidity on us. We have to stand up, knowing who we are and what we've been called to do. What is the gift and the call that is on your life? Stand firm on it, and God will stand with you.

OUR BLESSED ASSURANCE

In the days ahead, we must have a blessed assurance from God, not just that we're saved, but that we're called, that we are indeed His sent ones. We must know that we are called *"for such a time as this"* and that the purposes and plans of God are set in our hearts. That will give us the necessary boldness to face any enemy.

We have to know that we have heard from God, that the vision for which we are fighting came from Him and not from our own ideas. When that vision goes up on the flagpole, our spirit must be there saluting it. We have to know that even though we find ourselves in the midst of adversity and run into all sorts of problems and situations, that He is for us and He is with us. That produces the boldness this hour requires.

When everything that you've heard prophetically is different than what you're seeing in the natural, you have to know that God is in the deal and that He's the One who sent you to the other side. He knew that storm was coming, so don't become confused and think you have taken a wrong turn. He will take you safely across to the other side, and He will stay with you until the end.

Now is the time to be very bold and very courageous, for this is our time and our season! This is the season for the fulfillment of our promise. Step boldly into the promises you have from God. Set them up as a monument in your hearts so that, in the moment of conflict, when the waters of the Jordan are raging, you can know that God is able. Just be sure to build your monuments from the things God has said and done, not from the works of your own hands.

Our God is the Hope of Glory, and He will take us across to the other side. We are going to make it, so be bold.

A Victory Lap

What we are doing right now is running a victory lap. Get rid of your victim mentality, that escapism and that rescue mission mindset. This is a victory lap. The verdict is already in. We will live with God forever. That should give you all the boldness you require.

It doesn't really matter who's in the White House; it matters who is on the throne of our hearts. Jesus is the One, and He will finish the work He has begun in us, personally and corporately. So now is the time to be active, to be bold, to be courageous and to be impactful.

In the political arena, the tide has finally turned, and the winds of change are blowing. That wind is with us, it is for us, and it is blowing from the four corners of the earth. So now is the time to rise up! Now is the time to be bold! Now is the time to make the declarations and the proclamations that are necessary, politically, to begin to make our move.

TIME TO MAKE YOUR MOVE

There is a proper timing for every race. Whether it's a horse race or a relay race, there is a time to make your move, and now is that time. If you have something baking in the oven, prophetically this is the time for it to come out. This is the moment we've all been waiting for, so don't draw back now. Arise and shine. This is your moment.

Be bold! Be courageous! And let's take back everything that was taken from us, everything that was stolen. Boldly embrace the Lord right where you find Him, in that place of faith. When you can't see further ahead, boldly take another step, and you'll find that He is always there. Now is the time for boldness.

Chapter 11

Time for Change

But we all, with open face beholding as in a glass the glory of the Lord, are changed into the same image from glory to glory, even as by the Spirit of the Lord.　　　2 Corinthians 3:8

The Church has experienced many different revivals since 1948, when the Lord began its restoration, but we have now gone through a long season of drought. Those who have been moving in the Spirit, growing and building in this hour by the Spirit, have actually been building from the residue of what was yet in their hearts. But we are now getting ready for a new wave of revival.

THE REMNANT

What we have right now is a remnant from the last wave, but now we're about to see a brand new wave wash across the Body of Christ. When this wave begins to come forth, we will see a new generation arising. They have been praying for revival, but they don't really know what that revival will look like. They have heard what sounded so very good to them, but so far they have not tasted of the river themselves.

In the meantime, some have gotten a little drink of spiritual water and been refreshed, but they have not yet been a real part of a move of God, so they don't know the intensity of what God does when His glory enters any environment.

I Was in the Eye of the Storm

I was in the eye of the storm three different times, and I can tell you: when the Spirit of the Lord comes in, everything changes, including the ordering of your priorities.

When I was first saved, I had no desire to be involved in ministry. I was happy with what I was doing in business, and I enjoyed success at it, so I was comfortable where I was. The plan was that my son would eventually take over the business.

I had five companies and between two and three hundred employees, and no desire to do anything else. But when you come into the presence of the Lord, in the intensity of legitimate revival, everything changes. You can't realize just how all consuming it is unless you have been there and seen it. It's a great wave, and when that wave comes in, it sweeps away everything in its path.

Revival not only changes individuals; it also changes churches, cities and even whole nations. That mighty river comes rushing down, widening the river bed and taking everything in its path, and that's where we are headed right now. I have been blessed to see it and be changed by it, and it's coming again.

We started a church in Pensacola, Florida, and there we were able to sit with others who had experienced the Brownsville wave. Some of them have never left that season, and I have to say that I enjoyed that season very much myself. Some of my fondest memories were during that move of the Spirit and also the one I was blessed to witness and participate in as well in Ashland, Virginia.

When I was privileged to travel with Benny Hinn, I witnessed a move of evangelistic spirit like we hadn't tasted for a long time. If you look back into the late 1990s and the early 2000s, spiritually speaking, things seemed to be at their peak. But, believe me, the best is yet to come. It's on the way and getting closer every day.

Still, we have experienced a long drought now, and a lot of people have been patiently waiting for a new wave of revival to come. As they waited, they were touched, refreshed, renewed and some were legitimately revived and healed.

THE SKY WAS BLUER AND CLEARER

When revival came to me and I was touched by the Spirit, suddenly the sky was bluer and clearer, and there was an absolutely incredible grace on my life. It didn't matter what people said—if they insulted me, ignored me or rebuked—nothing mattered. I was in a little bubble of God's glory. God was everywhere around me and filling every space in me. If trouble was to come, He promised to be with me, even in the valley of the shadow of death, and He has been faithful to that promise and has been with me even in difficult moments.

All of us experience moments of trial, tribulation, struggle and disappointment. That's just life, and there is no reason to deny it. The good news is that God is preparing to release His blessing over us in an astonishing way in the midst of the greatest darkness that's ever been released in the earth. Gross darkness is now covering the earth, but God is about to hit us with blessings that will "knock our socks off," as the old saying goes.

In the release of God's glory, we will recover everything that has been stolen from us. It may not all come back in the same form, but if not, it will come in a greater form and in a greater way. It may not come back in relationships with the same people, in the same situation (for instance, the same career), but it will be greater than what we lost because this coming wave is going to be greater. Now is the time! God is turning us upside down so that we will finally be right side up. He's doing it politically, in our nations, and He's doing it in the Church. Everything begins, first and foremost, with us.

THE TIME FOR CHANGE

Now is the time for change, transition and transformation. And it's happening right before our eyes. It's not just happening on the streets; it's happening in our hearts. It's not just happening in the church; it's happening in our hearts. It's not just happening in the nations of the world; it's happening in our hearts. We must be open and willing to change, for

God is taking us from change to transition to transformation.

God wants to change our mindset so that we can begin to move into our destiny. We have to be prepared to take that next step. Everything that can be shaken will be shaken, but that which remains shall be part of the Kingdom. Prepare yourself for transformation, to transform in transition into this Kingdom experience.

Get out of the Church mindset and get into the Kingdom experience, and begin to walk that blessing out because now is the time!

NOW IS THE TIME

Now is the time to release apostolic mandates through the media. Now is the time to be strong and influential in every part of our society and in all areas of influence, but particularly in the area of media. Be bold with each one of your ministries and don't be afraid to promote others!

All who have a 501(c)3 certificate know that the first article says "To promote the Gospel of Jesus Christ." Don't be afraid to promote it, but promote it righteously and biblically.

Time for Change

Now is the time to make declarations and proclamations. We push back the darkness with those prophetic declarations and proclamations, but we must undergird our declarations and proclamations with intercessory prayer.

What a wonderful and amazing season we are in! This is a season like no other season that we've been in from the very beginning of time. This is the time to walk it out. Now is the time for change.

My Vision

In 2017, I had a vision. In the vision, I was standing with a crowd of people on a very small platform, posing for a photograph. I felt someone or something poking me, and when I looked up, I saw that a group of young people had arrived, and they all wanted to be in the photo too.

Through this vision the Holy Spirit was telling me that I needed to make room for the next generation to come in, to hear them and to know their heart. We must not think that we will convert the new generation to our way. We have had our season, and this is now their season. We must be ready to open the door of our hearts to them and to open our ears to hear them. Are you ready to see what God is about to do?

The Lord said to me that day, "This is not the time to pose; this is the time to press in and press on for everything that I have for you." So, don't pose, wait, stop or hesitate. This is the time to press into God. He is doing something very dramatic, something very amazing. We are now coming to the end of a season and stepping into an extremely blessed new time. Now is the time for change.

Chapter 12

Time for Unity

Holy Father, keep through thine own name those whom thou hast given me, that they may be one, as we are. John 17:11

This is a time for unity, and we will soon see barriers falling between races. Traditional barriers are coming down, as are cultural barriers, denominational barriers and national barriers,

Prepare your heart because there will be some strange bedfellows beginning to come together in this hour, as God begins to separate the sheep from the goats. This separation comes at harvest time. You may be surprised who the Lord pairs you with in harvest.

Trust God that He knows the hearts of all men of all nations. He is even now weighing our hearts each and every day, with each and every decision we make. It is a strategic and prophetic moment.

THE STRANGE BEDFELLOWS

As the strange bedfellows emerge, you will see people coming into your life that you never expected to have a relationship with. At the same time, some that you expected to be connected to forever will suddenly depart. Don't panic. It's all part of the season we're in.

It will take great wisdom to know who is who in the days ahead because you can't tell from the outward appearance or from the things people say or do. Let the Lord weed your garden by testing every heart.

Today we need wisdom and discernment more than ever before. God said:

> *Wisdom is the principal thing; therefore get wisdom: and with all thy getting get understanding.* Proverbs 4:7

That same chapter adds:

> *Keep thy heart with all diligence; for out of it are the issues of life.* Proverbs 4:23

Right now, more than anything else, we need to guard our heart because everything flows out from it. All of us will experience offense, trauma, hurt, pain, sadness, sorrow, disappointment and frustration. We must learn to quickly unload the baggage and free ourselves of the problems. Set aside all of the weighty issues that hold you back. You cannot afford to be burdened by them because now is the time for unity.

NOW IS THE TIME FOR GREATER UNITY

Now is the time for greater unity, and unity begins in the House of the Lord. Unity is the prelude to the great blessings that are on their way, the prelude to the great harvest that's coming.

Be assured that we are on the threshold of the greatest harvest ever known to man, but, at the same time, we are on the threshold of the greatest battle ever known to man. It's all because of the season we're in.

If, in the days to come, you hear a prophetic voice crying out, "Peace, peace," run from that voice. This is not a time for peace; it is a time for war. This is the end time. It is time for all warriors and end-time handmaidens to rise up and be who they are called to be. However, we must not be fighting each other but our common enemy.

MOLDED IN THE FURNACE OF ADVERSITY

This is a very special season, and God has been working on our hearts for a long time now. The heart of a true leader is molded in the furnace of adversity, and many of us have gone through adversity in the last twenty-four to thirty-six months. Many of us have indeed gone through the most difficult times and seasons of our lives. But now is the time to unite for the fight.

This is the moment. Things that seemed like they were gone forever—lost, past, over—God will suddenly restore. Get ready for it. God will make a way where there is no way because He is the Way-maker! He can unite us.

The unity that is needed at this time must begin with apostles and prophets. We have to learn how to walk together and how to work together. We have to learn how to work our way through problems, circumstances, situations and differences. We can't just walk away from each other; we have to learn to walk through situations together, looking past our differences and into the depths of the hearts of men and women. God's Kingdom is not made up of bricks and mortar, but of lively stones.

BUILDING IN A MAN OR WOMAN
IS BUILDING THE KINGDOM

When we build into a man or woman of God, we are building God's Kingdom. His Kingdom is not about a big building, a big ministry or a big name. What we want to build is inside of men and women, for God's Kingdom is within them.

It all starts with unity. That is the prelude. The apostle and the prophet must walk together. We are to be prophetically influenced and apostolically led. It's time for the war horse and the eagle to work together. That's the very heartbeat of God.

We need to be able to see into the distance and into the future, not just where God was and now is, but also where He is headed. I want to kiss the things that He's kissing, do the things that He's doing. I want to be in the right place at the right time doing the right thing, so I need to know the heartbeat of God as never before. And His heart is for unity.

The prophetic companies of the future will be of many different streams, but the great stream that is being released in this hour is like that of John the Revelator. John had great intimacy with God. He laid his head upon the bosom of Jesus, so that he could know the very heartbeat of God.

163

There is a prophetic generation being raised up that will walk with the apostolic generation. The prophets will be like John the Revelator, and the apostles will be like the sons of Issachar who knew what it was that Israel was supposed to do, so that we can all walk as one.

TIME FOR VISIONARIES

It's a time for visionaries to rise up among us! There's a big difference between a dreamer and a visionary. The dreamer dreams big dreams, and we've heard from many of them. They go from one big dream to the next. A visionary wakes up and makes dreams become a reality. They take a dream from revelation to mission, from mission to strategy and from strategy to action. What we need to do today is put boots on the ground, convert our vision into a practical strategy and walk it out into the fulfillment of the promise that God has put upon our lives, and we have to do it together.

Every prophetic word comes with an obligation and responsibility for the one who receives it. We can't just leave God's promises up there in Lollipop Land. So many people are just bouncing off of the walls, and sooner or later you have to come down, put your boots on the ground and be able to walk this thing out. You have to be able to do the deal, and now is the time. Like never before, now is the time. Walk it out together.

WALKING AND WORKING TOGETHER

It's not just about the apostles and prophets, but about the entire five-fold ministry walking and working together, realizing and respecting the gifts and call of God on their lives. But it does start with the apostles and prophets; they are the foundation. The House that God is now building, this end-time army, must have a solid foundation of the apostolic and prophetic.

You and I must know who we are and what we are called to do in this hour. There is one right place of alignment for us, and we need to get into it. All of the shaking that's going on all around the world is for the purpose of end-time alignment. It is to put us in the right place, doing the right thing, connected with the right people, knowing who we are and what we are called to do in the Body of Christ.

OUR PRIMARY PURPOSE

Our primary purpose is to raise up, build up, equip, empower and launch God's people. He is turning His Church upside down so that it will be right side up. When He is finished, the leaders will be where they belong, on the bottom, sending others out, launching them forth, having first empowered and equipped them. That will be a joyous day for all. Now is the time for unity.

Chapter 13

Time for Intercession

I exhort therefore, that, first of all, supplications, prayers, intercessions, and giving of thanks, be made for all men; for kings, and for all that are in authority; that we may lead a quiet and peaceable life in all godliness and honesty. For this is good and acceptable in the sight of God our Saviour; who will have all men to be saved, and to come unto the knowledge of the truth.

1 Timothy 2:1-4

Intercession is an important subject for the end-times. My primary calling is that of an intercessor. In fact, that was the first in-church ministry God gave me when He took me out of the market-place ministry now more than twenty years ago, in 1997. I heard about what was happening in Pensacola and decided to leave all and join the revival. So, my first ministry and my primary calling is that of a prophetic intercessor.

I believe that any true prophet must be an intercessor. Any five-fold minister, if he or she is not an intercessor, a person willing to cry out and intercede for the people, should not be in the ministry at all. If you're a pastor and you're not crying out and interceding for your people, then you don't have a right to pastor them, for you don't have a shepherd's heart. Intercession is the first gifting and calling of any five-fold ministry.

LEARNING WHAT INTERCESSION IS

When I first went to Brownsville, I didn't know what intercession was. Oh, I had my own personal prayer life and it was strong, but I didn't yet understand what an intercessor was, having come out of a traditional church. It was Lila Terhune who taught me what intercession was, and this became such an important part of my ministry that I was placed on the intercessory prayer team in Brownsville and was part of the prayer team that prayed at the end of each service. It was a wonderful opportunity for me to minister in that way during the Brownsville Revival.

A PERIOD OF TURMOIL

Before that revival broke out, Pastor Kilpatrick and his people had built a new sanctuary. But the church experienced a period of turmoil in which some people left the church, and it was because Pastor Kilpatrick had made the decision to stop having programs and started having prayer meetings. Some were upset that he was going after God. This was so important to him that he determined to either have revival or be taken home to Glory. The Lord had warned him that he would lose hundreds, perhaps even thousands of people, but he was determined to go after God anyway.

A prophet came to the church and saw in a vision the new building with hundreds of honey combs dripping honey off of the sides of the roof. Sister Lila felt that this was meaningful because her ministry was all about cross pollination.

Lila came to visit us in Canada in 2017, and while she was there, she, her armor bearer and I went to Niagara Falls. It was a very nice day, although it was a little windy. Suddenly some bees appeared and one stung me on the ear. When she heard about it, she said, "Everywhere I go, bees come." I believed that the bee stinging me on the ear was the impartation

I had been waiting for. When God taps you on the shoulder to do something new in life, it may sting a little. It will cost you something, and it's bound to bring you some pain. But it will also bring great gain.

God is trying to change the way we hear, the way we see and the way we think. He has moved many times and in many different ways in my life to move me to another level, and it always seems to have a little bite with it. So, if you have been going through something like that, don't worry about it. It's your time.

I Keep an Eye on the News of the Day

As an intercessor, I try to keep an eye on the news to see what is happening in other countries, and what I see doesn't look good. If you follow the politics of the day, you know what I mean by that. Some of the things that are happening here in North America are also happening all over the earth. Great change is coming. This requires our intercession. Now is the time for intercession.

Chapter 14

Time for Waiting Upon the Lord

But they that wait upon the LORD shall renew their strength; they shall mount up with wings as eagles; they shall run, and not be weary; and they shall walk, and not faint. Isaiah 40:31

This is a life scripture that the Lord has given me so that I can overcome and become what He has ordained me to be. This promise never leaves my heart because I can't make the journey without it. I need this rock-solid assurance.

Sometimes we have a problem with the timing of things—the delays and the detours. We always want things to happen immediately, and God has His own timetable. I battle a lack of patience, and I'm sure you do too. Like you, I want to know why I don't have God's promise already. If He said it's mine, then where is it? I want it. I fight for it, contending for it, but then I settle down to listen to God's heart. He always knows best.

Not a Passive Waiting

The secret, of course, is waiting on the Lord for the right timing. But this is not a passive waiting, as many imagine. When the disciples of Jesus tarried in the Upper Room in Jerusalem, they were not in a passive position. They were obeying Christ's command to wait and were actively seeking His timing. They were rewarded with the outpouring that came on the Day of Pentecost

Tarrying or waiting on God is an active force. You are pressing into His fullness as you await His promise. If you're not careful, the delays, detours and disappointments, combined with your lack of patience, can knock you out of the box. You have to trust God's goodness and know that His timing is always best. It's worth waiting for.

You have to learn how to overcome life's disappointments. The prophet Habakkuk said:

I will stand upon my watch, and set me upon the tower, and will watch to see what he will

*say unto me, and what I shall answer when I
am reproved.*   Habakkuk 2:1

The prophet was being totally transparent. When
he said, *"I will stand upon my watch,"* he was using
a military term. He was being vigilant, waiting and
anticipating God's instructions and meditating on
what his response to God should be. And it worked;
the Lord responded to him:

> *And the LORD answered me, and said, Write the
> vision, and make it plain upon tables, that he
> may run that readeth it. For the vision is yet for
> an appointed time, but at the end it shall speak,
> and not lie: though it tarry, wait for it; because
> it will surely come, it will not tarry. Behold, his
> soul which is lifted up is not upright in him: but
> the just shall live by his faith.*
>   Habakkuk 2:2-4

Often, the vision seems (to us, at least) to be tar-
rying, but God said it would *not* tarry. It is *"for an
appointed time,"* and God knows what that time is.
We often don't know the right timing. God says,
"Wait for it!" Why? *"Because it will surely come"* and
"it will not tarry."

Even though, to us, it seems to be late, it's not late at all. God is an on-time God. He was on time for the men and women of old, and He will be on time for us too.

GOD KNOWS THE PERFECT TIMING

God knows the perfect timing for everything. The things He has prepared for us are *"for an appointed time,"* and, since He is the one who appointed them, He knows the proper timing. He is always right on time.

Often, we get ahead of God, and even more often we get behind Him. He is always on time. He is not usually early, but He is also never late. I must wait on Him. I must give Him time to process things in my heart. If I take off as a first response and jump on out ahead of God, I may get my machinery clogged up with a lot of other people's input—their problems, their circumstances, their situations and their negativity—and then I can't process things properly. I need to be careful who and what I listen to because faith comes by hearing, and so does doubt, contention, strife and division, and all of these can hinder me. I need to get quiet in God's presence, wait on Him and hear what He has to say about any given situation.

LISTENING TO IDLE GOSSIP HURTS US

Listening to idle gossip hurts us and gets us knocked off track, causing us to miss our call—all because we listened to someone else's nonsense. Get firmly planted in a faith-filled environment where there is a spirit of unity, so that your seed can begin to grow. Be careful about the people you associate with and the type of people you follow. Make sure they're going where you're going, or you may end up being someplace you don't want to be. I'm referring to friends and family members and also to your close inter-acting spiritual relationships. You need to sort through them, or they will affect your ability to answer the call of God on your life. Most important of all, spend quality time in the presence of God and learn to hear His voice. Wait on God.

KNOW WHO YOU ARE IN CHRIST

Many times, when we hear a prophetic word being given, we wonder, "Could that really be me?" We need to know who we are in Christ by revelation. And, more importantly, we need to know who Christ is in us. He is the Hope of Glory.

When we begin to think on all of our weaknesses and shortcomings, the thought quickly dawns on us, "I can't do that." If we listen to what Mom, Dad and other people say about us, we will be discouraged. Thoughts of our inadequacies only lead us to mediocrity, and that's dangerous. Who wants to be *"neither cold nor hot"* (Revelation 3:15-16)? Personally, I want to be red hot and right in the middle of what God is doing. Let Him hand you the ball, and then you run with it. That requires that I spend time in His presence, waiting on Him.

Oh, I don't have the most talent, the most ability or the most intellect. In my senior class in high school, I was the least likely to do anything spiritual or to succeed at anything. But that was fifty years ago, and I wonder what my classmates would think or say if they could see me now. Waiting in God's presence pays off.

"WHAT COULD TURN A DEVIL LIKE YOU INTO AN ANGEL?"

Before my aunt went to be with the Lord, she called me one day. She had heard that I was in the ministry and asked, "What could turn a devil like you into an angel?" It was a fair question. The answer was, "Jesus, Him and Him alone." You just need a touch from God. That's the only thing that can turn your life around. The glory of God, the power and the presence of God made manifest in your heart and life fully and wholly will do the trick. Get into His presence, and receive His touch.

When we hear a great prophetic promise, we do tend to ask, "Could that really be me?" When this happens, I have to take some action. I can't just sit there and ponder on that thought, or I will own it. I have to fight the thought. God said in His Word:

> *(For the weapons of our warfare are not carnal, but mighty through God to the pulling down of strong holds;) casting down imaginations, and every high thing that exalteth itself against the knowledge of God, and bringing into captivity every thought to the obedience of Christ.*
> 2 Corinthians 10:4-5

Pull down those strongholds and cast down those vain imaginations. You have to deal with them, for this is where the battle begins. Let the very thoughts of God fill your mind and heart as you wait in His presence.

When the devil attacked Jesus in a monumental battle, it was at the site known as "the place of the skull." And that is where he will fight you too, in your head. You have to win this battle of thoughts. Thoughts are just events that have not yet manifested, and you have to deal with them before they do.

Sometimes it's the devil who plants a bad seed there, and sometimes it's your own imagination. Whatever the case, you have to deal with those seeds before they become strong weeds. If powerful seeds take root and grow, then you must take an axe to the root of them and get them out.

Therefore, you have to know how to fight in the Spirit with the blood of the Lamb, the power of the cross, and the declarations and proclamations of the Word of God. These will root out any negative activity that is trying to change the way you think and ultimately change the way you act. This is urgent because the outcome will alter your destiny. We have to fight back, for we cannot allow ourselves to fall into a state of double-mindedness. Spend more time in God's presence, and you will know His thoughts.

STEPHEN'S TESTIMONY

Acts 6 records the story of Stephen, the first Christian martyr, as he was being stoned to death. He said:

Time for Waiting Upon the Lord

*Behold, I see the heavens opened, and the Son of
man standing on the right hand of God.*

Acts 7:56

The Lord stood for Stephen, and He will stand for
you too. The Lord showed up for the three men in
the fiery furnace (see Daniel 3:24-25), and He'll show
up for you too. He has no choice, for He is God, and
He can't do it any other way. We must learn to trust
Him in every furnace experience, for the making
and molding of a true leader for God occurs in the
furnace of adversity. That's where we are tried and
proven, and God will show up for you there if you
have spent quality time in His presence. He is a good
and faithful God.

Unfortunately, sometimes we run out of patience
and give up. If we have tried something once or
twice, and there is no apparent result, we begin to
think that we're all alone.

CONSIDER PETER

Consider Peter: He was with Jesus for three and
a half years and had seen all of the miracles, signs
and wonders that Jesus did. Then He saw men take
Jesus captive, hang Him on a cross and mock and

torture Him. He saw Jesus take His last breath and give up the ghost. Soon afterward, Peter said to the other disciples, "Let's go fishing" (see John 21:3), and they all went back to their old business.

Why did this happen? Because Peter was disappointed and discouraged. Things hadn't worked out as he imagined they would. But no matter what you have gone through, God knows all about it. He also knows that all men sin and fall short of the glory of God. In His mercy, grace and love, He is there to pick you up, restore your hope and strength, and give you another chance. Wait on Him.

CONSIDER ELIJAH

Consider Elijah. He sent his servant out to see what God had promised him would happen, and six times the man came back with a negative report. He had seen nothing at all. On the seventh time, however, the servant saw a cloud the size of a man's hand. Elijah knew this was God's answer, so he declared it. He had to declare it before it came to pass. We don't wait to declare something until it has already happened. We must declare it before it is ever seen or, perhaps, even imagined.

If something does not seem to be working for you, go back again and again. Don't stop just because the devil is bothering you and you want him to stop. You need God, and the devil will never relent. He is determined to rob you of your destiny. You can either keep moving with God or you can sit still. It's harder to hit a moving target, so I'd rather be a moving target than a sitting duck. Wait on the Lord.

ABRAHAM'S TRIALS

Abraham went through many trials because he was ahead of his time. In the same way, God's best has been reserved for you and me. I haven't tasted it yet, but I know it's coming. God spared you and me for this particular moment in time. Therefore, you must shake yourself, cleanse yourself of all wrong thinking and start to deal with the truth that Christ has spoken into your heart. If He said it, He can do it, and He can do it through you.

God did it for Abraham and Sarah. Abraham buried his father on the edge of the Promised Land and then had to deal with his nephew Lot and separate from him before he could come into the Promised Land. And every single one of us has to deal with our Lot. You have to exercise your faith and trust in the Lord through "come what may." Get your mindset changed and have a new way of looking at things.

Why isn't it happening? Well, for sure we're not waiting for God. He is waiting on us. It's time to fight for the truth so that the power of truth can overtake the powers that are manifesting today. God will do this through us, His Body, as we learn to wait in His presence.

STAND IN FAITH AND WAIT

We are to do everything that we can possibly do and then stand in faith and wait for God to do as only He can do. Until it happens, we must be watching as we wait:

Watch therefore, for ye know neither the day nor the hour wherein the Son of man cometh.
Matthew 25:13

Our watching serves several purposes. We are to watch for the enemy, watch for those who come in as wolves in sheep's clothing, false prophets, come to lead us astray. We must let no one deceive us. We must put our face to the ground and our hand to the plow, so that when Christ appears we are found doing what He told us to do. Then, we can rejoice at His coming.

Time for Waiting Upon the Lord

Some say, "Well, I'm just waiting on God." That can't be true. God is waiting on you, and while He waits, He's watching everything you do. He's waiting for you to make the right choices in life and align yourself with His will.

The sooner you step into that place, the better. The sooner you cast aside the things of this world, the better. The sooner you pull down all vain imaginations, the better. The sooner you tear down the strongholds that keep you from doing His will, the better. Let's get down to business because the clock is ticking. It's time to realize that God is waiting on us.

Chapter 15

Time for a Response

I will stand upon my watch, and set me upon the tower, and will watch to see what he will say unto me, and what I shall answer when I am reproved. Habakkuk 2:1

We must respond to the truth when we hear it. That's why it is important for us to preach the truth, just as it is important that we all hear the truth, as faith comes by hearing (see Romans 10:17).

HOW SHOULD WE REACT?

How should we react to God's signs? It's one thing for such a sign to appear and for us to acknowledge it, but it is another thing altogether for us to have the proper response, to take the necessary action.

How does God want me to respond to what He

is showing me? The prophet Habakkuk wrote: *"I will ... watch to see what he will say unto me, and what I shall answer when I am reproved."* There is a proper response, and we must find it.

As prophets of God, we must ask Him, "What do You want me to do with this revelation? Give me the wisdom to know." In short, we can say that God wants us each to consecrate ourselves to our particular call, answering that call, and separating ourselves from all else so that we do not become entangled in or distracted by what's happening in the world around us.

The things of this world are here today and gone tomorrow, so stop wasting your time with them. The world is like wind that passes and like grass that withers away. When we are tried by fire, what is temporal will all disintegrate and go up in smoke. If you get caught up in all of these things, you will never answer your call.

The devil will say to you, "You have plenty of time. Don't worry about spiritual things until you are much older. The demon that he is, then he will torment you by saying, "Oh, you have missed your day because you waited too long." The truth is that *this* is your day. If you are eighteen, eighty or one hundred and eight, this is your day. Now is your time to respond.

WHAT HAS GOD CALLED YOU TO?

What has God called you to? You might think that you will be a bricklayer in Heaven, working on those glorious streets? But, no, your calling is for the here and now, and these are the days of the harvest. Refuse to sit on the sidelines while harvesting is going on all around you.

Jesus wasn't a farmer, but He knows about a harvest and calls us to know it too. If you and I do not participate in this end-time harvest, it will be a shame. Jesus said to His disciples:

> *The harvest truly is plenteous, but the labourers are few; pray ye therefore the Lord of the harvest, that he will send forth labourers into his harvest.* Matthew 9:37-38

Those laborers need to know that the time to harvest is now.

In 2017, I was led to preach this for many months, especially to challenge Christian leaders. They needed to know what dispensation we are living in and to react to it properly.

Paul taught the Corinthian believers:

Time for a Response

For if the trumpet give an uncertain sound, who shall prepare himself to the battle?
There are, it may be, so many kinds of voices in the world, and none of them is without signification. Therefore if I know not the meaning of the voice, I shall be unto him that speaketh a barbarian, and he that speaketh shall be a barbarian unto me.

1 Corinthians 14:8 and 10-11

We are to blow the trumpet and sound the alarm. There is no shortage of voices in the world, and they all have significance, but we must blow the trumpet, making a clear sound so that people know how to respond, know what God expects of them in this hour.

THE TRUE PROPHETIC MESSAGE OF THE HOUR

"Now is the time" is the true prophetic message of the hour, and we must respond to it. Step in, step up and step out. Wake up, arise and advance.

On New Year's Eve of 2018, I prophesied this message, and I also did so on the closing night of the International Coalition of Prophets Conference in Dallas, Texas in November of 2017. "What time is it?" I asked the participants and then answered my own question: "NOW is the time for you and me."

When you finally see Jesus, you will never be able to say, "I didn't know." You might respond, "I wasn't sure about that, God," but He will answer, "Just so that you would know for sure, I blew a trumpet in Heaven that declared, The Kingdom is birthing a new dimension, and I am sending forth the armies of God."

In September of 2017 the entire universe converged to make the announcement on the Feast of Trumpets, so that you would never have an excuse. What you do with that knowledge is between you and God. Personally, I see myself on the threshold of a lot of things in the Kingdom. God has given me many revelations over recent months, and they have turned me upside down and inside out, touching my roots to reach my destiny.

Please don't allow the voice of reason to rob you of your greatest blessing. Trying to figure everything out in your natural mind is not the answer. God wants us to bind our minds to the mind of Christ so we can think in the supernatural realm. Why? Because He's bringing the supernatural into the earth and making it seem the most natural thing. How can He do that if we continue to think with the natural mind?

Time for a Response

Our responses must reflect faith in and obedience to what God is saying. No matter what revelation comes to us, with it comes responsibility. I've received a revelation from God. Now, what do I do with it? How do I respond?

PAUL'S GREAT CONFESSION

As I noted early on in the book, Paul's great confession before King Agrippa is one that I desperately want to have before the Lord. He said, *"I was not disobedient unto the heavenly vision"* (Acts 26:19). We must be faithful to the vision, faithful to the revelation. If God speaks to you, you must respond appropriately.

So, how do we respond to God? If you're an end-time warrior, do you just keep doing the same thing you've been doing? According to God's Word, these last days will be like the days of Noah. In other words, people will just go about the business of their daily lives, as if everything is fine. I want to tell you that it is not fine in the spiritual realm. There's a war going on, and you must be obedient to the Spirit in this hour. You must position yourself correctly and have the correct heart attitude if you expect to fulfill your destiny, the call of God that's on your life. Don't wait for someone else to position you. Do it yourself.

HOW WILL YOU RESPOND?

Do you really believe that these are, in fact, the last days and that you are a part of the end-time army? Do you really believe that you were born *"for such a time as this"*? What does it all mean? What do we have to do? How do we react? Where do we position ourselves? What is God trying to say to us? If the army of God, made up of the true sons and daughters of God, is being birthed in this hour, what should we look like and how are we to respond?

Let's take a closer look at what Paul told Timothy in this regard. When he wrote to his spiritual son Timothy, he was in the middle of some severe trials and tribulation and was transitioning into a place of legacy. What he wrote to Timothy is so profound that there can be no doubt that it was for more than Timothy in the first century B.C. It was also for you and me today. He said:

> *This know also, that in the last days perilous times shall come. For men shall be lovers of their own selves, covetous, boasters, proud, blas-*

phemers, disobedient to parents, unthankful, unholy, without natural affection, trucebreakers, false accusers, incontinent, fierce, despisers of those that are good, traitors, heady, highminded, lovers of pleasures more than lovers of God; having a form of godliness, but denying the power thereof: from such turn away.

2 Timothy 3:1-5

We can all see this manifesting today in the political arena, in the governmental arena and in the education arena all over North America. But don't think for a moment that what we're seeing here in the U.S. and Canada is unique. This problem is worldwide.

As Christians, we must take a stand against the ungodly liberalism that is sweeping our world. This will put us in the crosshairs of persecution, but so be it. We are being tested, and we must chose Christ and His way and stand tall for the Judeo-Christian values that have made our part of the world great.

There is now war in every arena of business, government and education. We will either do battle or we won't. Whose side are we on? The plumbline is dropping, and we have a serious decision to make. Don't wait. Now is the time for a response. If you don't make a decision now, your opportunity will pass. Many will miss the day of their visitation.

ALL THAT LIVE GODLY SHALL SUFFER PERSECUTION

After clearly describing the times we are living in, Paul went on to speak of his own persecutions:

> *But thou hast fully known my doctrine, manner of life, purpose, faith, longsuffering, charity, patience, persecutions, afflictions, which came unto me at Antioch, at Iconium, at Lystra; what persecutions I endured: but out of them all the Lord delivered me. Yea, and all that will live godly in Christ Jesus shall suffer persecution.*
> 2 Timothy 3:10-12

Paul endured and was delivered by the Lord, but, he warned: *"all that live godly in Christ Jesus shall suffer persecution."* We are even now moving into a season of great persecution, even as we see these other end-time phenomena that were declared to Timothy. Therefore these words are a declaration to us too.

Later, in chapter 4, Paul charged Timothy to go forth boldly and proclaim the Gospel, the Good

News, to preach God's Word. He exhorted Timothy to step into this legacy moment in his life.

In chapter 2 of Second Timothy, Paul tells us how we should respond to this moment in time. When we see Jesus face to face, we will not be able to say that we were never warned. He has spoken through His prophets and through great signs in the heavens, so we have no excuse. When you come face to face with Him, He will try your works, be they good or evil. And there is no in-between, no gray area, except in the mind of man. This is what Paul said about it:

> *Thou therefore, my son, be strong in the grace that is in Christ Jesus. And the things that thou hast heard of me among many witnesses, the same commit thou to faithful men, who shall be able to teach others also. Thou therefore endure hardness, as a good soldier of Jesus Christ.*
>
> 2 Timothy 2:1-3

Paul was saying, "Remember what I have told you and commit it to others you are responsible for." Are you a pastor, a leader, a teacher or a prophet? Then respond as Paul tells us here. Deliver the message of God. Don't candy-coat it because the time is too short. It's time to declare the truth because only the truth will set people free.

We are to *"endure hardness as a good soldier of Jesus Christ."* Do you want to be His soldier? Then get ready for hardship and face it valiantly:

> *No man that warreth entangleth himself with the affairs of this life; that he may please him who hath chosen him to be a soldier.*
>
> 2 Timothy 2:4

That's clear enough. Don't entangle yourself with the things of this world because there's a call on your life, and that call is eternal:

> *And if a man also strive for masteries, yet is he not crowned, except he strive lawfully. The husbandman that laboureth must be first partaker of the fruits. Consider what I say; and the Lord give thee understanding in all things.*
>
> 2 Timothy 2:7

Having the revelation is not enough. We have to know how to respond. This is not an accidental moment. This is a moment in time when God is blowing the trumpet, to let His army know that it is time to arise and shine. The Message translation says it this way:

> *So, my son, throw yourself into this work for Christ. Pass on what you heard from me ... to reliable leaders who are competent to teach others. When the going gets rough, take it on the chin with the rest of us, the way Jesus did. A soldier on duty doesn't get caught up in making deals at the marketplace. He concentrates on carrying out orders. An athlete who refuses to play by the rules will never get anywhere. It's the diligent farmer who gets the produce. Think it over. God will make it all plain.* 2 Timothy 2:1-7, MSG

One day, while I was lying down resting, I saw a row of big harvesters lined up to work. I said, "Lord, don't pass me by. I'm going to throw myself in front of these harvest machines so I don't miss You." He saved me for this moment. He spared me for now, so I'm not about to miss the harvest. I must respond.

IF YOU MISS THE HARVEST, IT'S BECAUSE YOU HAVE CHOSEN TO

If you miss the harvest, it's because you have chosen to. I intend to throw myself in front of the harvesters. That's what Paul told Timothy to do. He said, *"Throw yourself into this work for Christ. Pass on what you heard from me."*

Expect opposition. *"Take it on the chin just like Jesus did,"* Paul said. Why? Because great blessing comes in the midst of persecution. Stop the nonsense and the fairy tales. I'm all for holy laughter, but not all the fooling around I see going on in churches today.

There's a big difference between holy laughter and some of the nonsense people are doing. The proof is the way they are living their lives. They are not good examples for others to follow.

"A soldier on duty," Paul wrote, *"doesn't get caught up in making deals at the market place. He concentrates on carrying out his orders. An athlete who refuses to play by the rules will never get anywhere. It's the diligent farmer who gets the produce. Think it over. God will make it all plain."* He couldn't have made it more plain, and He can't possibly make it more plain than the signs He has placed in the heavens for all of us to see.

Paul continued:

> *Fix this picture firmly in your mind: Jesus, descended from the line of David, raised from the dead. It's what you've heard from me all along. It's what I'm sitting in jail for right now—but God's Word isn't in jail! That's why I stick it*

*out here—so that everyone God calls will get in
on the salvation of Christ in all its glory. This
is a sure thing:*
If we die with him, we'll live with him;
If we stick it out with him, we'll rule with him;
*If we turn our backs on him, he'll turn his back
on us;*
If we give up on him, he does not give up—
 for there's no way he can be false to himself.
                                    2 Timothy 2:8-13, MSG

Do you want resurrection power? Sooner or later
you have to die to self. You have to die to your own
dreams, your own hopes, your own deals. You have
to die to the things going on around you. And now's
the time. In your heart, come to a place of reality and
respond to God.

Forget about others for a moment and concentrate
on your own need. The One who knows all things
is surely right there beside you, and this is between
you and Him. If you believe that you are called to be
a soldier of God, and you're willing to do what Paul
told Timothy about what a good soldier does, now
is the time. God made covenant with man from the
beginning, and He's still a covenant-making and cov-
enant-keeping God. How will you respond to Him?

Don't be concerned about making a vow; be concerned about breaking a vow. All Heaven is watching you right now, as you make your decision for God.

Do you believe that we are we in the last days, that this is our moment, that it is your moment? Are you really called as a soldier, an end-time warrior, an end-time hand-maiden of the Lord? Are you legitimate? Did He really die for you? If so, are you willing to die for Him? Are you willing to go the distance? Are you willing to fight the fight and run the race? If you are, let Him know your heart. Show Him your intentions. Tell Him right now, "I will go, Lord. Send me. I'll do it. I'm in." Respond to Him.

Tell Him you are determined to be all the way in, not half way in. Tell Him you are determined not to become entangled in the things of this world, that you're going to do what a good soldier does. Tell Him now with your heart what you're willing to do because it's time to pick up our cross and follow Him daily. Respond well, for now is the time for a response.

Chapter 16

Time to Embrace the Cross

But we preach Christ crucified, unto the Jews a stumblingblock, and unto the Greeks foolishness; but unto them which are called, both Jews and Greeks, Christ the power of God, and the wisdom of God. Because the foolishness of God is wiser than men; and the weakness of God is stronger than men. 1 Corinthians 1:23-25

Don't try to look beyond the cross for some other solution. The cross is our only hope. We have none other.

I am so sure this is true that I am determined to embrace the cross every single day and in every possible way. I want to pick up my cross and carry it. The cross of Christ is the place I go to get right today, and it will continue to be the place I go to get right every day.

We have to come to grips with ourselves, activate our faith, defeat those negative things that are going on inside of us, grab hold of our carnal thoughts and ideas and destroy them at the root. We have to understand the power of the blood of Jesus Christ to wash away those thoughts and ideas and apply His blood to our minds, by faith, by declaration, by proclamation and by demonstration. It is time to embrace the cross.

ELIJAH'S ALTAR

When the prophet Elijah came on the scene, he built an altar, and every great prophet builds altars. Next, Elijah put a sacrifice on his altar. In the New Testament, the altar is our heart, and the sacrifice God is looking for is us picking up the cross. As our example, He gave His all, sacrificing His only begotten Son on that cross. Jesus was the Lamb of God, our great Sacrifice.

Today men hate the cross and want to tear it down because it was God's altar of sacrifice, and the sad thing is that we are letting them do it. Even church people are trying to leave the cross behind, but Jesus said that we needed to pick it up and follow His example. He does not invite us to follow Him without carrying our cross. So, pick up the cross, and then follow Him.

The cross is your only hope; there is none other. The cross represents the legitimate sacrifice of Christ made for you and me. It was God's altar, and it represents the greatest victory for all of mankind.

If there is no cross, then there is no resurrection. Today we all want resurrection without first dying the death of the cross. There is power in the cross— power to heal, power to save, and power to deliver. The Church has lost its power because its members have left the foundational truths and refuse to build an altar in their own heart. Build an altar in your home, but first build an altar in your own heart. It's time to embrace the cross.

CHOOSE THIS DAY

In Elijah's time, the prophets of Baal built their altar, and then the people were challenged with a black and white choice, just as they had been in Joshua's day. Joshua had said:

Choose you this day whom ye will serve.
                                        Joshua 24:15

Today Christ is with us, and He is saying, "Build an altar in your heart to Me. Go back to the cross and get your life right. Don't buy into the oft-repeated lies of this day. Seek the truth in your adversity. Now is the time to open your heart to Me. Forget about everything up to now, and build an altar in your heart right now. Go to the cross today. Take anything in your life that is in violation of the Scriptures, and bring it to Me. Take anything that is contrary to My will and leave it at the Cross."

THE PROMISED FORGIVENESS

Jesus died so that we would have forgiveness of sins. Confess them now, for He will not hold them over our head. Then, if you sin again, confess it, and He will forgive you again. His blood was shed for you, and that is your remedy.

Right now take your sin to God. Humble yourself before Him. He has promised:

> *The sacrifices of God are a broken spirit: a broken and a contrite heart, O God, thou wilt not despise.* Psalm 51:17

Humble yourself before Him now, and if there's something you want Him to remove from your life, something ungodly or distracting in your life, give it to Him now. Embrace the cross.

GRACE WAS NOT MEANT AS A LICENSE TO SIN

Grace was never meant to be license to sin, but rather, a remedy for sin, so that we can overcome. The only way to access grace is to humble yourself before God. He resists, or opposes, the proud but gives grace to the humble (see James 4:6).

There are sins of commission and sins of omission. Anything ungodly that you have tolerated is a sin. That time that you spent doing something else when you could have been advancing the Kingdom of God, that was a sin. Those times that you compromised in your heart when you knew what you were doing wasn't the right thing, that was a sin. God said:

Therefore to him that knoweth to do good, and doeth it not, to him it is sin. James 4:17

Let Him wash away all sin right now. Leave it at the cross.

Now is the time to re-dedicate yourself to Him, to Him alone, to His will, to His purpose, to His Kingdom. He wants to give us a brand new start and a brand new heart. He wants to take that heart of stone out and put in a heart of flesh.

David was said to be *"a man after [God's] own heart"* (1 Samuel 13:14). Right now you are choosing to turn away from everything else and to turn to God. Follow after Him, and let His will be done. Let His Kingdom come into your life. Accomplish it by embracing the cross as never before. Now is the time to embrace true grace through the cross.

Chapter 17

Time to Lay Aside Carnal Reasoning

The Lord knoweth the thoughts of the wise, that they are vain. 1 Corinthians 3:20

If God has taught me anything, it's that there is a great difference between being led by the Spirit and led by the natural, by the voice of reason. He told me recently in a prophetic word not to allow the voice of reason to rob me of my greatest blessings. Reason will do exactly that, and you'll end up figuring your way out of the greatest blessings ever. God wants to take you beyond the natural and into the supernatural.

In these end-times, there will be a massive release of revelation knowledge and a massive release of end-time prophecy. Of course, the enemy will attempt to insert his two cents worth, so we must test every spirit. Don't receive what is not of God.

THERE IS NO SHORTAGE OF VOICES

There are others who, even though their revelation is good, don't know prophetically how to bring it forth. There is no shortage of voices, and, as we have previously noted, Paul wrote to the Corinthians, *"none of them is without meaning"* (1 Corinthians 14:10, NIV). The problem is that not everything builds up the Church.

When you blow a trumpet sound, make sure it's a clear sound so that people know how to respond. You also need to know how He wants you to respond. Because we are living by faith, our response will normally be contrary to our mind, will and emotions. It will not reflect what I like to do or what I think is right to do. My mind, will and emotions make up my soul, but God wants us, His sons and daughters, to be led by the Spirit of God, not by our soul. Too many times we try to figure things out, but when we do that, we figure ourselves out of a great blessing, sometimes the greatest of blessings.

REVOLUTIONIZING MY PERSONAL LIFE

For some time now, God has been speaking to me things that are revolutionizing my personal life. He has been confronting me with things I didn't want to do. He said to me, "I want to take you back to your future." That was not my deal. My thought has always been: *Don't look back! Go forward!* But God has confronted me with truth that I could not deny. He is showing me that if we want to reach our destiny, we have to touch our roots. I had been prophesying that for quite a while, but when we prophesy, we're prophesying to ourselves first of all. When you preach prophetically, you're preaching to yourself first.

Then the enemy will come and test you to see whether or not you are willing to walk in what God is saying. In that moment, we must not allow the voice of reason to rob us of our greatest blessings.

DIFFICULT FOR ME

What God has been saying has been difficult for me. I was a businessman, and I wanted to hear $2 + 2 = 4$. I always want to figure things out. I have a ten-year plan, a plan for each day and a to-do list for tomorrow. I want everything to be as clear as $2 + 2 = 4$, but sometimes, in the Kingdom of God, $2 + 2 = 22$. I have to learn to count the way God counts. He has a different view, and my mind, will and emotions—my soul—wars with the Spirit.

I don't have to worry about the enemy; he's under my feet. It's me that I have to deal with every day, bringing myself into alignment with the revelation God has for my life. I have to know the times and the seasons, not just for the Body of Christ as a whole, but for myself in particular.

SOMETIMES PROPHETS SEE BETTER FOR OTHERS THAN FOR THEMSELVES

Sometimes prophets can see the future for everyone else but have trouble finding it for themselves. When one prophet meets another, he says, "You're fine, but how am I?"

The battle I'm going through is the same battle you're going through. Don't think that when I say to you, "Now is the time for change, transition, and transformation," that I'm talking to you only and not to myself too. I'm going through a transformation at the very root of who I am. The moment we stop changing we stop growing and start dying. I'm looking for life not death. And if I'm looking for life, I have to be willing to change. That includes changing my way of thinking.

What God has been saying to me is this: "If you are to fulfill your destiny, you will not just have to accept change and embrace change, you will have to fall in love with change." I am now in a new season of life. I went through a very difficult time physically, but the Lord healed me wonderfully, and I'm strong and going forward. But I'm now being challenged in other ways.

DON'T LIVE BY YOUR
INTELLECT OR EMOTIONS

God didn't design us to live by our intellect or our emotions. Who are the true sons of God? Those who are led by His Spirit. Far too many in the Body of Christ are being led by their emotions or by their thoughts (or someone else's) and not by the Spirit of the Lord. Each of us must be able to hear the voice of the Spirit for ourselves. We need to know what He's doing and what it feels like to embrace the fullness of who Christ is in us. To do it, we must ignore our own feelings.

Our spiritual battle will end only when God's trumpet sounds and we are taken home to be with the Lord. Until then, fight for all you're worth. The good news is that I have read the end of the Book, and we win. But things will get a lot worse before they get better. Each battle we face will prepare us for the battle of all battles.

Many Christians today live with constant feelings of guilt. They feel bad about all the conflict around them and think they should somehow have been able to resolve every conflict. Only our Lord Jesus Christ can do that.

Knowing that we all serve the Lord of the Harvest keeps us concentrating on His harvest fields. Get bold with your sickle. Keep your tools sharp and ready to reap at any moment. It's time to lay aside carnal reasoning.

Chapter 18

Time to Let God Be God

For he will finish the work, and cut it short in righteousness: because a short work will the Lord make upon the earth.   Romans 9:28

What an amazing time this is! God is doing a quick work and accelerating everything. What before took months and years is now being done in hours and days. What took hours and days before is now being accomplished in seconds and split seconds. Don't lose out in this unique season.

For me, the hardest part about doing something good for the Lord these days is keeping my big nose out of things. I am always wanting to fix things, but He doesn't need my help. In David's day, when an otherwise good man put out his hand to steady the cart that carried the Ark of the Lord, the man was instantly struck dead. Every time you get the idea to fix things for God, remember that it would be far better if you just stayed out of it. Just concentrate on getting closer to God and developing a healthy fear or reverence of Him, and let Him do the work.

ATTN: ALPHA MALES AND DOMINANT FEMALES

Some of the alpha males and dominant females among us need to learn this important lesson. Give God space to work, and He will do it in His season. And this is the season! No matter what things look like on the surface, no matter what the governments of the world are doing at the moment, and no matter how bad the educational system looks, no matter what is currently going on in the Middle East, or on the Korean Peninsula, this is God's season, and His promises are never failing. He said:

> *And we know that all things work together for good to them that love God, to them who are the called according to his purpose.* Romans 8:28

That promise is just as true today as it ever has been. In the meantime, God is accelerating His timetable, and we are moving ever closer to the prophetic moment that every prophet foresaw.

Time to Let God Be God

For many months now, I have been led to warn God's people that we are nearing the end. This truth has long been in my heart, and I have long studied it. Now I feel that the time has come to release what He has shown me and share it more with others.

MOVE ON

In years gone by, we were preaching on the restoration of the Church and the day of the saints. Now we must concentrate on the end-times so that we can see the prophetic unfolding. As prophets, we have prophesied one thing, but now we must move on to another. God doesn't stay in one place. He moves on, and we must move on with Him.

This is the reason prophets must keep pace with God and stay on the cutting edge of what He is currently saying and doing. We are called to our generation to be agents of change, but there is no way we can be agents for change if we ourselves are unwilling to change and be changed. We always want to change others, but that's not how it works.

When we get married, we quickly want to change our mate, but the only one we can change is ourselves. So, what's the use of me preaching and prophesying change to others if I'm not willing to be changed myself? If I am to help others change, I must live a life of change. If I am to help others to be willing to pull up stakes and follow the cloud of God's glory, then I must be its first follower. Let God be God.

KEEP UP WITH THE CLOUD

Prophets are on an exciting journey, and we must keep up with the movement of the cloud. We can't afford to pitch our tent and settle down in one place. We are called as pioneers and pilgrims on this way. We are headed somewhere, and we have to be prepared to move when God moves, to do what He does and say what He says.

This can sometimes be a great challenge, and some of us have been misunderstood because of our prophetic gifting. How we feel and what we are saying often does not fit in with the accepted trends of the day, and others become uncomfortable around us, wanting us to conform. Personally, I can't concern myself with all of that. I have to keep myself in a position to please God. If I try to please Mr. World or even Mr. Church, I quickly become a man-pleaser rather than a God-pleaser.

Sometimes we have to declare things that are hurtful to others or difficult for them to swallow. But our duty, as servants of God, is to speak the truth, regardless of who it hurts. We have people wanting us to prophesy about their latest love affair or that person they now think they're called to marry, and this can be very challenging. That's why prophets need a lot of prayer, and then they need to declare to others what God is saying to them, not what any individual wants to hear. It's time to let God Be God.

Part III

Things that Must Happen Before Jesus Comes

Chapter 19

The Great Falling Away (Apostasy)

Let no man deceive you by any means: for that
day shall not come, except there come a falling
away first.   2 Thessalonians 2:3

One of the things that must happen before Jesus comes (and it's happening), is the apostasy of many. This is the great falling away spoken of in the Scriptures.

As an example, there is no comparison between the Christianity of fifty years ago in North America and the Christianity of today. In those days, churches were full, and the people in them were living their faith. They were hungry for the things of God and were living by the Judeo-Christian values that laid the foundations for our nations.

Today, not only are Christians falling away from the church; many of them are turning on the church and attacking it. The church is under attack, not only from without, but also from within. I feel sorry for those who are doing the attacking because God loves His Church and will come back for His Bride. How would you like it if someone attacked your bride? Well, that's just how Jesus feels.

CHRIST REBUKES AND CHASTENS HIS OWN

This doesn't mean that Christ will not confront the Bride and change her where she needs to be changed. He will, and He does. He is even now saying to His Bride:

> *Those whom I love I rebuke and discipline. So be earnest and repent.* Revelation 3:19

But even though the Lord rebukes and disciplines His people, He will not permit others to attack His Bride. When Peter was preaching to the thousands who had gathered after a lame man began walking in Acts 3, he said:

> *Repent ye therefore, and be converted, that your sins may be blotted out, when the times of refreshing shall come from the presence of the Lord. And he*

shall send Jesus Christ, which before was preached unto you: whom the heaven must receive until the times of restitution of all things, which God hath spoken by the mouth of all his holy prophets since the world began. Acts 3:19-21

This is still Christ's message to us today. He is coming, so get ready. In the meantime, society is trying to push Jesus and all Judeo-Christian values out and replace them with New Age ideas. Everything is now acceptable, we are all brothers and sisters, and all religions lead to Heaven. But that's simply not true. We can only be brothers if we have the same Father, only those who are washed by the blood of the Lamb are born again from above, and there is salvation in no other name than the name of Jesus.

Why are these truths so important? Because those who don't have Truth will die. Believing the Gospel is a matter of life and death—YOUR life or YOUR death. It is the difference between Heaven and Hell. It will determine our eternity.

Apostasy Is Nothing New

Refuse to be part of the apostasy, the great falling away of our time. Apostasy is nothing new, but this is the greatest apostasy of all times. This current apostasy will release us into the final days and, just as the tide of faith moves out, it will then come rushing back in. Be sure that when it happens you have your boat in the water because a rising tide floats all boats. Yes, we have seen the falling away, and it is growing, but there will also be a new wave of God's glory sweeping over us. Don't miss it.

THE UNPRECEDENTED KILLING OF BABIES

Part of the apostasy of our day is the unprecedented killing of unborn babies. Every day we shed innocent blood and continue to make laws that contradict the clear teachings of the Word of God. Aside from killing newborns, we are also poisoning our children who live. How can it be possible that children are now allowed to watch pornography so that they will develop "safe sex habits?" May God help us.

DEFINING APOSTASY

Wikipedia, the online encyclopedia, defines apostasy in the following way: "Apostasy is the formal disaffiliation from, or abandonment or renunciation of a religion by a person. It can also be defined within the broader context of embracing an opinion contrary to one's previous beliefs." Wake up, people! It's here.

This didn't happen in our grandparents' day or even our parents' day. But it *is* happening now, and that should cause every one of us to wake up and shake ourselves. This is not a time to shrink back. Stand up against evil. The wise King Solomon wrote:

> *Remember now thy Creator in the days of thy youth, while the evil days come not, nor the years draw nigh, when thou shalt say, I have no pleasure in them.* Ecclesiastes 12:1

Remember now!
Paul wrote to his son in the faith:

> *For the Spirit God gave us does not make us timid, but gives us power, love and self-discipline.* 2 Timothy 1:7

It is the bold who will take the Kingdom in these days. Get ready. Our risen Lord will soon come riding on His white horse. He will have fire in His eyes and a scepter in His hand, and He's coming back to rule and reign. We are not called to be wimps. We are called to take dominion and rule and reign with Him.

THE WORLD NOW SEES US AS TROUBLEMAKERS

Part of the apostasy of our time is that the world now sees us, the members of the Body of Christ, as troublemakers. This should not surprise us. When King Ahab faced Elijah, he accused him of being *"the troubler of Israel"*:

> When he [Ahab] *saw Elijah, he said to him, "Is that you, you troubler of Israel?"*
> *"I have not made trouble for Israel," Elijah replied. "But you and your father's family have. You have abandoned the LORD's commands and have followed the Baals.*
>
> 1 Kings 18:17-18, NIV

Does it sound familiar? The Ahabs and Jezebels of our day are doing the same.

THE SPIRIT OF DECEPTION

The great falling away has come because of something Jesus foretold in Matthew 24:

The Great Falling Away (Apostasy)

And Jesus answered and said unto them, Take heed that no man deceive you. Matthew 24:4

Today, more than ever before, a spirit of deception is attacking the church. Verse 24 of that same chapter declares:

For there shall arise false Christs, and false prophets, and shall shew great signs and wonders; insomuch that, if it were possible, they shall deceive the very elect. Matthew 24:24

In this new season many of the *"elect"* are indeed falling away, just as Jesus prophesied. He went on from verse 4:

For many shall come in my name, saying, I am Christ; and shall deceive many. And ye shall hear of wars and rumours of wars: see that ye be not troubled: for all these things must come to pass, but the end is not yet.

Matthew 24:5-6

Jesus told us not to be afraid, but, rather, to be in faith. All of this will happen before the end comes. He went on:

For nation shall rise against nation, and kingdom against kingdom: and there shall be famines, and pestilences, and earthquakes, in divers places. All these are the beginning of sorrows. Matthew 24:7-8

These things are happening, but they are only *"the beginning of sorrows."* So, that's where we are, at the prelude, on the doorstep of the season of sorrows, which speaks of a tribulation period. This is just the beginning of it.

Then, in verses 12 and 13, Jesus said:

And because iniquity shall abound, the love of many shall wax cold. But he that shall endure unto the end, the same shall be saved.

Matthew 24:12-13

This speaks again of the great end-time apostasy, the falling away from Christ, His Kingdom and His principles. It is happening right now, and it is one of the greatest signs of the end time. It has been in progress for the past twenty-five years or more.

ANOTHER DEFINITION

Another definition of this word *apostasy* is "an act of refusing to continue to follow, obey or recognize a religious faith." It can also be "the abandonment of a previous loyalty or defection of a spiritual way." Just look at the statistics and look at the churches. Twenty-five years ago they were filled, and today they are not. This is due to an apostasy, a falling away from our spiritual roots. The Church is under attack from the outside and from the inside.

There are even prophetic voices that are attacking the Body of Christ and the local church. I don't want to have anything to do with those who are condemning the Church. Yes, we need conviction and we need challenge to the place of change, but we do not need to be condemned.

THE APOSTASY IS NOW DEEPLY ROOTED

This apostasy is not just in the church. It has reached into the very root system of our North American society. Again, it doesn't really matter who is in the White House; what matters is who is on the throne of our hearts. You cannot regulate immorality, and today there has been a falling away from Christ and from our Judeo-Christian values and foundation, and that has resulted in a loss of moral values.

Again, the biggest problem in this regard is the issue of abortion. Every year we are killing millions of babies, and there is no way to justify this killing of innocents still in the womb. There is nothing in the Bible that could ever justify such action. To kill an unborn child is an insult to the living God.

Anything that we do to help this situation seems just to be cutting the top of the hedge. It will grow right back out. The only thing we can do now is take an axe to the root, and the root is apostasy, a falling away from Christ and from our Judeo-Christian principles. This affects our homes, our families, our businesses, our towns and cities, and our nations. Our only hope is a mighty move of the Spirit of God. God's people must rise up and manifest the presence and the power of God.

WHAT WE NEED TO KNOW

This apostasy, this falling away, that is part of the end-time fulfillment of what needs to happen before Christ comes back, and God wants you and I to facilitate change, to shift the atmosphere the same way He told the original apostles to do when they came to Him and pleaded, *"Teach us to pray"* (Luke 11:1). These disciples didn't ask Jesus how to do miracles, how to feed the hungry or how to preach. But, seeing that His prayers were effective and what

He asked for came to pass, they asked Him to teach them to pray. His answer was, Pray like this: *"Thy kingdom come, thy will be done in earth as it is in heaven"* (Luke 11:2). We should be praying that prayer every single day. This is bringing Heaven to Earth, and it will happen, but it will only happen in God's way and in His time.

GOD IS CALLING US TO THE POLITICAL ARENA

For years now, our political systems have been separating us more and more from God. For this reason, God is calling His people into the political arena, to make decisions and choices for the people based on their faith in Jesus Christ. We need men and women in politics today who know they are not just there for a political appointment but for a divine appointment. They must be ministers of God in politics. God is calling some of us to get out of the boat and get into that arena, not just to complain about what the other side is doing, but to make a legitimate difference.

Paul was accused by some of the Jews in Jerusalem of causing apostasy among their people (see Acts 21:21). He knew what real apostasy was and wrote to the Thessalonian believers:

Now we beseech you, brethren, by the coming of our Lord Jesus Christ, and by our gathering together unto him, that ye be not soon shaken in mind, or be troubled, neither by spirit, nor by word, nor by letter as from us, as that the day of Christ is at hand. Let no man deceive you by any means: for that day shall not come, except there come a falling away first, and that man of sin be revealed, the son of perdition; who opposeth and exalteth himself above all that is called God, or that is worshipped; so that he as God sitteth in the temple of God, shewing himself that he is God. 2 Thessalonians 2:1-4

As previously noted in an earlier chapter, Paul warned his spiritual son Timothy:

This know also, that in the last days perilous times shall come. For men shall be lovers of their own selves, covetous, boasters, proud, blasphemers, disobedient to parents, unthankful, unholy, without natural affection, trucebreakers, false accusers, incontinent, fierce, despisers of those that are good, traitors, heady, highminded, lovers of pleasures more than lovers of

The Great Falling Away (Apostasy)

God; having a form of godliness, but denying the power thereof: from such turn away.

2 Timothy 3:1-5

Jude also warned of apostasy in his epistle to the churches:

Beloved, when I gave all diligence to write unto you of the common salvation, it was needful for me to write unto you, and exhort you that ye should earnestly contend for the faith which was once delivered unto the saints. For there are certain men crept in unawares, who were before of old ordained to this condemnation, ungodly men, turning the grace of our God into lasciviousness, and denying the only Lord God, and our Lord Jesus Christ. Jude 1:3-4

Before the second coming of Christ, there will be an increase in this falling away, and then *"the man of sin"* will be revealed. I believe that he is already in the earth today but has not yet been revealed. The chaos and anarchy in the world today is from the spirit of anti-Christ, manifesting total rebellion. When people who seem normal during the day then go out to the streets at night and go wild, calling good evil and evil good and doing all sorts of damage to life and property, that is the spirit of Anti-Christ.

These are all signs of the end times. This is a time of apostasy, of falling away, of attack on the Body of Christ, attack on the local church on the outside and on the inside. Our society is being attacked and eroded on every side, taking the church out of the picture and removing the name of Jesus from all activities.

The Ten Commandments are being removed everywhere as irrelevant. But these are the foundations of our faith, along with the blood and the power of the cross. We have stood back powerless and watched all of this happen. But God is calling us to be His voice, His hands, and His feet to our generation.

JESUS WAS A GREAT REVOLUTIONARY

Jesus was a great revolutionary, and if you are a follower of Jesus Christ, you are called to be a revolutionary too. We are not called to a spirit of timidity, but to be bold and courageous and make our voices heard. We must take a stand: "You will not take Jesus out of any part of our life or society, for He is our Lord and Savior."

The Great Falling Away (Apostasy)

Because Jesus was a revolutionary, if you're not a revolutionary, then you might be following someone else. All of the early apostles were revolutionaries. They did not preach a seeker-friendly gospel. A seeker-friendly gospel would not have cost Jesus His life, and it would not have cost them their lives either. They were crucified upside down, dragged through the streets, persecuted and slain for His name's sake. Today we worry about someone being mad at us, so we shut up, and evil prevails. The only way that evil can prevail is for good men and women to remain silent. We need to rise up and speak up, not shut up.

THE THREAT OF LOSING OUR TAX-EXEMPT STATUS

We get so worried about politicians taking away our non-profit status, but the last time I checked that was not a criteria for entering the Kingdom of Heaven. When I stand before God, He will not ask me, "How did you make out with your non-profit status?" Those worries are strictly from the flesh and have nothing to do with salvation and following Jesus. If you are willing to remain silent, you may know *about* my Lord, but you can't really know

Him. When you know Him, His heart becomes your heart, His will becomes your will, and His voice becomes your voice. Then you will begin manifesting the presence and the power of God in your area of influence.

Be careful when people begin to say good things about you. The world is at odds with God and His people. If they are saying good things about you, you have to wonder what side you are really on.

THE FAITH ONCE DELIVERED TO THE SAINTS

The apostasy of our age is a departure from *"the faith that was once delivered to the saints,"* and we are to *"earnestly contend"* for it once again.

The apostates of our age includes two types of people:

1. Those who have knowingly turned away from Christ and no longer even pretend to be Christians, and
2. Those who still claim to be Christians but have departed from the true faith.

This latter group can also be divided into two subgroups:

The Great Falling Away (Apostasy)

1. Those who are deliberately twisting the Scriptures and perverting the Gospel to draw disciples away from Christ, and
2. Those who endorse false teaching because they want to share in the fame, power and wealth it brings.

Where do you stand?

Chapter 20

A Rapture

For the Lord himself shall descend from heaven with a shout, with the voice of the archangel, and with the trump of God: and the dead in Christ shall rise first: then we which are alive and remain shall be caught up together with them in the clouds, to meet the Lord in the air: and so shall we ever be with the Lord. Wherefore comfort one another with these words.

1 Thessalonians 4:16-18

There will be a rapture, or snatching away. I will leave it to you to decide if it will be pre-trib, mid-trib or post-trib. What I'm sure of is that it is coming.

This should not surprise us. Elijah was raptured in Old Testament times:

A Rapture

And it came to pass, as they still went on, and talked, that, behold, there appeared a chariot of fire, and horses of fire, and parted them both asunder; and Elijah went up by a whirlwind into heaven. 2 Kings 2:11

Jesus Himself was raptured in the sight of His disciples:

So then after the Lord had spoken unto them, he was received up into heaven, and sat on the right hand of God. Mark 16:19

And when he had spoken these things, while they beheld, he was taken up; and a cloud received him out of their sight. Acts 1:9

There were other raptures, and there will be more raptures other than the rapture of the Church, notably those who are saved during tribulation.

When will it all happen? Just be sure you're ready when it does.

Chapter 21

The Rebuilding of the Temple in Jerusalem

But in the last days it shall come to pass, that the mountain of the house of the LORD shall be established in the top of the mountains, and it shall be exalted above the hills; and people shall flow unto it.   Micah 4:1

I believe, scripturally, that before Christ comes back the Jewish people will locate the Ark of the Covenant, and this will lead to the rebuilding of the Temple in Jerusalem. Some might ask, "Why would they want that old ark; they can just make a new one?" Well, that's not the way it works. The Ark is eternal.

I have been to the Third Temple Institute in Jerusalem and can tell you that Orthodox Jews are assembling materials and making plans for the eventual rebuilding of the Temple. It will not be a replica of the original Temple, or the Second Temple that existed in Jesus' day. It will be an entirely new temple. They call it the Third Temple.

We have just stepped into the third and final reformation, which is the restoration of all things. During this process, every promise for the Jewish people will be yea and amen, and every promise for the Church will be yea and amen. We are now headed toward a parallel harvest that will include both the Church and the nation of Israel.

EARLY IN THE MORNING OF THE THIRD DAY

As noted earlier, biblically, we are living early in the morning of the third day from the time Jesus was born, for the Bible declares that with God a day is like a thousand years. What happened on the morning of the third day? That was when Jesus was raised from the dead. This says to me that the Body of Christ, the Church, is about to rise up in resurrection power and become what we were called to be. It is time to walk in Kingdom destiny and power. Rise up in the power and presence of God. Rise up in His glory.

Even now, a serious archeological effort is underway to locate the Ark, and if anyone can find it, the Jewish people can. It is amazing how much history they have uncovered in recent years. My feeling is that they know where the Ark is and will soon recover it. In the meantime, the people of the Third Temple Institute are busy preparing everything that will be needed for Temple worship and sacrifice.

A restored Jewish Sanhedrin is already meeting, and everything is being put into place so that once the construction begins on the temple, it will not take long. Then they will reinstitute Temple worship with all of its complexity. This Third Temple will be built before Jesus comes. When you receive notice that a shovel has been put into the ground, get ready. Things will happen very quickly.

The enemy knows (as do Israel's natural enemies), and they, too, are awaiting their Messiah (the Antichrist). The moment the shovels are thrust into the ground to begin the rebuilding of the Temple, everything will break loose, and the enemy will set in motion anything he can to hinder it. He will not be successful. The Temple will be rebuilt, as Micah foretold:

Why will this be done? So that God's people can flow into it and be discipled:

The Rebuilding of the Temple in Jerusalem

And many nations shall come, and say, Come, and let us go up to the mountain of the LORD, and to the house of the God of Jacob; and he will teach us of his ways, and we will walk in his paths: for the law shall go forth of Zion, and the word of the LORD from Jerusalem. Micah 4:2

Is this something we should be worried about? No, just make sure you're ready for what is to come!

Chapter 22

The Revealing of the Antichrist

Let no man deceive you by any means: for that day shall not come, except ... that man of sin be revealed, the son of perdition; who opposeth and exalteth himself above all that is called God, or that is worshipped; so that he as God sitteth in the temple of God, shewing himself that he is God.   3 Thessalonians 2:3-4

Another thing that has to happen before Jesus comes is the unveiling or revealing of the Antichrist. As I noted earlier in the book I personally believe that he has already been born. Why do I say that? Because the spirit of Antichrist, the spirit of chaos, has already been released in the earth. That is the reason we are experiencing anarchy and chaos all over the world. But the Antichrist himself is yet to be revealed, so we don't yet know who he is.

The Revealing of the Antichrist

At first, everyone will think that the Antichrist has come to save the world, to bring peace. But while everyone is reaching out for that peace, he will turn the tables, turning against Israel and against God. He will oppose God and insist that *he* be worshiped as god. That is why he is called the Antichrist, and he must be revealed before the second coming of Christ. What do you need to do about all of this? Just get ready for it.

Chapter 23

Tribulation

And one of the elders answered, saying unto me, What are these which are arrayed in white robes? and whence came they? And I said unto him, Sir, thou knowest. And he said to me, These are they which came out of great tribulation, and have washed their robes, and made them white in the blood of the Lamb.

Revelation 7:13-14

Tribulation is another thing that must happen before Jesus comes. Some are prophesying that we are already in the tribulation. What craziness is that? What we are currently experiencing is *not* the tribulation. When the tribulation comes, believe me you will know it.

As I have said before, there will be three and a half years of tribulation that are nearly intolerable and then there will be three and a half years that are absolutely intolerable. There will be seven years of tribulation, and what we are now seeing is not the tribulation.

Some are prophesying that what we are experiencing now is already Heaven. This is Heaven? If this is Heaven, we have been ripped off. I can tell you assuredly that this is *not* Heaven. Heaven will be wonderful beyond your wildest dreams.

TRIBULATION COULD BEGIN AT ANY MOMENT

As noted, there are at least seven or eight things that have to happen before the second coming of Christ, but nothing has to happen for tribulation to come. It could start immediately.

What will the tribulation look like? The Scriptures describe it as looking like nuclear or chemical warfare, or the use of what we now call "weapons of mass destruction." I can't say for sure what it will look like, but I do know that according to the timetable of God, nothing else has to happen before it comes. One stupid move by some deranged individual could easily set it off.

In my humble opinion, from reading the Scriptures, I believe that tribulation will go on for a long period of time before the second coming of Christ, for this is one of the definite signs spoken of in Matthew 24 that point us to these events.

Why is it important to dwell on these things? Because if you are one of those who are fooling around, doing the wrong things at the wrong time, you need to be warned. If you don't take the time to read any other parts of the Bible, please read Matthew 24. It's a gold mine of information on the end times.

THE SETTING FOR THIS TEACHING

What was the setting for this teaching? Jesus was sitting with His early disciples, the first apostles. In the book of Revelation, Jesus called the original disciples *"the apostles of the Lamb"* (Revelation 21:14, NIV). Matthew 24 begins this way:

> *And Jesus went out, and departed from the temple: and his disciples came to him for to shew him the buildings of the temple. And Jesus said unto them, See ye not all these things? verily I say unto you, There shall not be left here one stone upon another, that shall not be thrown down.*
> *And as he sat upon the mount of Olives, the disciples came unto him privately, saying, Tell*

*us, when shall these things be? and what shall
be the sign of thy coming, and of the end of the
world?* Matthew 24:1-3

This shows the early disciples already understood
that Jesus would come again. Their concern was to
be ready for His coming, so they asked Him what
they should look for. Again, He began His answer
in verse 4:

*And Jesus answered and said unto them, Take
heed that no man deceive you.* Matthew 24:4

So, the first sign of the end is a spirit of decep-
tion, and has there ever been a more powerful
spirit of deception at work than there is today? I
think not.

In the verses that follow, Jesus spoke of false
christs, wars and rumors of wars, nation rising
against nation and kingdom against kingdom, fam-
ines, pestilences and earthquakes in divers places.
These, He said, are not the end, but merely *"the
beginning of sorrows"* (Matthew 24:8). You need to
read through verse 15 at least to capture the whole
message.

Then, a little later in the chapter, Jesus said:

For then shall be great tribulation, such as was not since the beginning of the world to this time, no, nor ever shall be. And except those days should be shortened, there should no flesh be saved: but for the elect's sake those days shall be shortened. Matthew 24:21-22

Then, Jesus said:

Immediately after the tribulation of those days shall the sun be darkened, and the moon shall not give her light, and the stars shall fall from heaven, and the powers of the heavens shall be shaken: and then shall appear the sign of the Son of man in heaven: and then shall all the tribes of the earth mourn, and they shall see the Son of man coming in the clouds of heaven with power and great glory. And he shall send his angels with a great sound of a trumpet, and they shall gather together his elect from the four winds, from one end of heaven to the other.

Matthew 24:29-31

This will happen *"immediately after the tribulation of those days."* That tribulation will be so severe that *"except those days should be shortened, there should no flesh be saved."*

248

Tribulation

This tribulation was also foretold in Daniel 9 and 12 and Revelation 7 and 13. It is coming, and nothing else has to happen before it begins.

What we are experiencing right now is just a prelude to tribulation, the beginning of sorrows, a prelude to the end of time and proof that the rest will surely come.

Things will clearly get a whole lot worse before they get better. And, in the meantime, if someone is preaching peace, reject their message. They are not from God.

But just as there will be a beginning of tribulation, there will also be an end of it. Remain faithful and you will rule and reign with Christ. Are you ready for what is to come?

Chapter 24

The Great Harvest

And another angel came out of the temple, crying with a loud voice to him that sat on the cloud, Thrust in thy sickle, and reap: for the time is come for thee to reap; for the harvest of the earth is ripe.　　　Revelation 14:15

I have already mentioned this great harvest a number of times throughout the book. It will be the greatest harvest we have ever had in the history of the Church.

FOCUS ON THE HARVEST

There are a lot of different things going on all around us, and distraction is everywhere. Now, more than ever before, you and I need to focus, and our focus must be on the harvest.

The Great Harvest

The harvest is the thing that unites us. Even though we come from different streams, different backgrounds, maybe different ways of thinking, different denominations (and many more differences, including different cultures and traditions), the thing that we can all embrace is that now is the time for the harvest. The fields are white and ready.

Jesus is the Lord of the harvest, we are the children of the harvest, and these are the days of the harvest. So now is the time to grab that golden sickle and begin to reap. This is the time you have waited on for so long. You will now see the harvest you have long anticipated.

We are just now on the threshold of that great harvest, and the greatest day of the Church is yet to come. The mountain of the house of the Lord will be restored during the greatest harvest of souls yet.

In His Sermon on the Mount, Jesus said:

> *For verily I say unto you, Till heaven and earth pass, one jot or one tittle shall in no wise pass from the law, till all be fulfilled.*
>
> Matthew 5:18

God has to fulfill His Word, for He is God. He has to do what He said he would do.

And the most important thing that has to happen before Jesus comes back to rule is the great harvest. Although I don't have to worry about all of the details surrounding Jesus' return, the when or how to make it happen, I do have to be concerned about the harvest. This is my job, and this is your job. We are harvesters for Christ.

We have seen a great many different miraculous manifestations on the earth over the past fifteen years, and there is now an acceleration of signs and wonders happening both in the heavens and upon the earth. Be sure that your foundation is solid. If you are not standing on the Rock, Christ Jesus, then you have built your house upon the shifting sands.

Today, the whole earth is bearing witness to God's glory, and when things like this are happening on the earth and in the heavenlies, you need to ask yourself, "What time is it?" The answer is, Now is the time! Now is the time to make your move. Now is the time to get off of your seat. Now is the time to focus on the harvest. We all have a lot to do in a short span of time.

Part IV

Recent Events and What They Mean to Us

Chapter 25

What God Is Doing and Saying

Surely the Lord God will do nothing, but he revealeth his secret unto his servants the prophets.   Amos 3:7

As noted earlier in the book, in the spring of 2017 I began hearing a lot of talk about a sign in the sky that was expected to appear on Rosh Hashana. I felt a witness in my spirit that this revelation was true, but I didn't dare share it with others until I was sure, not just that it would take place, but more so, that I understood what it meant. What was God saying to us through this strange event?

I knew that the revelation in itself had no value beyond giving us goose bumps, if we didn't understand it, so I needed to hear from God. He spoke to me very specifically in the dream I described in Chapter 3. I saw a woman who was pregnant, and

I put my ear to her protruding belly and could hear the army of God marching. God told me that He was going to release a new dimension of His Kingdom and that the mature sons and daughters of Romans 8 would be released in the process. It was to be a birthing, a new beginning, a season of change and acceleration. The end-time army would now rise up.

I first released that word at the beginning of our summer camp in 2017, and once I had released it, the Lord spoke to me that in addition to that event, the year ahead was to be a year of the open door. Many doors would be opening to His people, and each time one of those doors opened, there would be a great shift in the Spirit world.

A Door Is Opened In December 2017

One of those doors opened on December 6, 2017. On that day Donald Trump did what no other American President had ever been bold enough to do. He publicly recognized Jerusalem as the capital of Israel and declared that the U.S. would be moving its embassy from Tel Aviv to Jerusalem. This put the U.S. firmly on the side of the sheep nations, friends of Israel. God showed me that this would result, not only in great prosperity, but it would also bring one flow of blessing after another.

I love much of what Donald Trump is doing for America, and I believe that what he has done by recognizing Jerusalem as the legitimate capital of Israel has set the stage for future blessings for this country and other allies of God's people.

After many centuries of exile for the Jewish people, Israel was recognized as an independent country in 1948. That has now been seventy years, but because of the many enemies surrounding that nation, with their constant threat to wipe her off of the map, no one was willing to recognize the legitimacy of her capital, and we, like many other nations, maintained our embassy in Tel Aviv.

Donald Trump not only recognized Jerusalem as the capital of the nation and began the proceedings to move our embassy there; he went so far as to declare Jerusalem as the "eternal capital of Israel!" That was a big deal, and it signified the dropping of the plumbline over the nations. God is separating the sheep from the goats and the sheep nations from the goat nations. The moment our president declared on our behalf that we are in alignment with Israel and that Jerusalem is her capital, something sounded in the heavenlies.

God loves Jerusalem. It is the only city in the world that He specifically told us to pray for, and He declared a blessing on us when we obey:

> *Pray for the peace of Jerusalem: they shall prosper that love thee.*   Psalm 122:6

Those who bless Israel will be blessed, and those who curse Israel will be cursed. We will be blessed because of what Donald Trump has done, and his actions will now spur the events of the end.

Until now, the Jews have not felt free to rebuild their Temple in Jerusalem because it was disputed territory. That is no longer the case. Donald Trump's declaration has put the U.S. firmly on the side of Israel, and when the U.S. flag was displayed alongside the flag of Israel on the walls of Jerusalem, people came from all over the world to see it and celebrate at the Wailing Wall, the only remaining part of Solomon's Temple. It was an historic event, and now the other events of the end time will fall into place very quickly.

There was much celebration in Tel Aviv, even though that city is now losing its mistaken distinction as the real capital of Israel and all of the diplomatic activity that distinction included. Now

Jews from any part of the earth can come to Jerusalem and worship their God. What an amazing moment!

This new alignment will bring financial blessing to America, and that will spill over into the Church. America and Americans will be blessed, and everything about America and Americans will be blessed in the process.

THE SHIFT OF FEBRUARY 2018

"Get ready for a door to open in February," the Lord said to me back in the spring of 2017. I understood that this door the Lord spoke of had to do with the raising up of His army and a great evangelistic trust that would result, but I didn't understand any other particulars of it or what might trigger it. Then, when it was announced, on the morning of February 21, 2018, by the family of the great evangelist Billy Graham, that he had passed away at the age of ninety-nine at his home in Montreat, North Carolina, I suddenly knew the significance of the Lord's words. Billy Graham's death was the triggering apparatus, and when the seed of his body went into the ground, there would spring forth a great harvest of evangelists. Evangelistic mantles would be dropped over the earth that day, to be picked up the whosoever wills who were prepared to answer the call of God to go into all the world and preach the Gospel to every creature.

On February 28, for the first time in history, a preacher of the Gospel was laid in state in the U.S. Capitol Rotunda, and there honored by a joint session of the U.S. Congress along with other dignitaries. Speakers that day included Senate Majority Leader Mitch McConnell, House of Representatives Speaker Paul Ryan, Vice President Mike Pence, and President Donald Trump. All of them thanked God for Rev. Graham and then praised his personal testimony and unique fruit. President Trump urged the nation to pray that God would raise up many more Billy Grahams to bless America and the world, exactly as the Lord had shown it to me.

MORE RECENT REVELATIONS

After the shift of February of 2018, the Lord showed me that change had accelerated and that nearly every month we would see something new and fresh for our people. For instance, He showed me that the lineup of Good Friday and Easter with

Passover this year was no coincidence, and that it represented another important shift.

In May, He said, we would experience another shift in the Spirit and then again, in July, a huge shift in the Spirit.

The Lord again cautioned me that this is a time of great deception, so we must remain alert. Even our government is under deception and is going after the puppets rather than the puppeteers. Syria, He told me, is only a puppet for Russia and North Korea is only a puppet for China. We should be going after the puppeteers instead of the puppets.

The Lord said that He is further dividing the sheep and the goat nations, that the end-time army would come from the north and east and that there would be an axis of evil and coalitions for good. He said He was separating the fields in a season of alignment not just by what men declare but by His testing of the hearts of men and the hearts of nations.

He further told me that Rosh Hashanah this year (2018) would bring in the Jewish year 5779, signifying the momentum for the fullness of the harvest. We have only begun to reap, and people are being aligned, empowered and equipped. The momentum we gain as we enter into a new year will take us into a deep place in the harvest.

GET READY

Get ready for acceleration and get ready for the blessings that will make acceleration possible. Miracles are on their way to us. Watch for them. Stop expecting the negative. Look for blessing to come your way. That is the faith walk. Stop expecting decline and prepare for advance. Stop expecting the worst and start preparing for the best.

I'm not saying that there will be no persecution in the days ahead. There will be plenty of persecution. Persecution comes with blessing. Jesus said:

> *But he shall receive an hundredfold now in this time, houses, and brethren, and sisters, and mothers, and children, and lands, with persecutions; and in the world to come eternal life.*   Mark 10:30

Blessing is coming, and persecution is coming with it because God is God, and He has to bless us now. He has no choice. He is bound by His promise. He is not like men, who promise and then don't deliver. He is not a man:

> *God is not a man, that he should lie; neither the son of man, that he should repent: hath he said,*

and shall he not do it? or hath he spoken, and shall he not make it good? Numbers 23:19

God can do nothing but bless us, so get ready to be blessed.

A Prayer for You to Pray

Please pray with me this prayer:

Lord, You see my heart and know my mind. I want to be Yours. You know the battle that I have been waging between the Spirit and the flesh. By the power of Your blood and by the power of Your love, wash away every stain, even pain, every sadness, every sorrow and every shame.

Lord, forgive me for my sins, the ones I have committed and the ones I have just considered. Forgive me for every sinful thought, every sinful word and every sinful deed. Wash me and make me new.

Now, Lord, show me the harvest field You have destined for me to reap. You said, "Whom shall I send?" I say, "Here am I; Lord, send me!"

Amen!

Author Contact Page

You may contact the author in the following ways:

By Email
bro.russ @ eagleworldwide.com

By Phone:
+1 905 308 9991

By Mail:
PO Box 39
Copetown ON L0R1J0
Canada

On Facebook:

facebook.com/eagleworldwide

facebook.com/russ.moyer.52

By visiting his website:
www.EagleWorldwide.com

EAGLE WORLDWIDE
RETREAT & REVIVAL CENTRE

SUMMER CAMP TENT REVIVAL

July through August
8 Powerful Weeks of Revival
Every Night @ 7:00pm

Specialty Schools
School of the Prophets
School of Freedom and Healing
School of the Supernatural

Location: 976 Hwy 52 Copetown ON   L0R 1J0
Call for more details   905 308 9991
www.EagleWorldwide.com

WINTER CAMP REVIVAL GLORY

February/March
10 Powerful Days of Revival Glory
Every Night @ 7:00pm

Specialty Schools
School of the Prophets

The Dwelling Place
7895 Pensacola Blvd Pensacola FL 32534
Call for more details   850 473 8255
www.TheDwellingPlaceChurch.org

EAGLE WORLDWIDE NETWORK

CREDENTIALING & SPIRITUALLY COVERING

Ministers
Marketplace Ministers
Traveling & Itinerant Ministers
Missionaries
Churches
Church Networks
Home Churches
Outreach Ministries
And more...

GOVERNING OFFICIAL
PASTOR MAVE MOYER

NETWORK COORDINATOR
PASTOR JOANNA ADAMS

CREDENTIALS AVAILABLE

Certified Practical Minister
Licensed Minister
Ordained Minister

OFFICE@EAGLEWORLDWIDE.COM

INTERNATIONAL COALITION
OF
PROPHETIC
LEADERS

THE INTERNATIONAL COALITION OF PROPHETIC LEADERS is an alliance of fivefold ministers operating in the office gift of the Prophet, from Ephesians 4:11-12, who have chosen to walk in covenant relationship with one another and in alignment with the apostolic movement.

Our primary interest is the restoration of the office gift of the Prophet and the gift of prophecy to the church with character, integrity and proper biblical protocol.

APOSTOLICALLY LED
& PROPHETICALLY
INFLUENCED

CPSIA information can be obtained
at www.ICGtesting.com
Printed in the USA
FFOW02n1534190718
47485277-50786FF